scarf
style 2

innovative
to traditional,
26 fresh designs
to knit

ann budd

INTERWEAVE
interweave.com

Technical Editor Lori Gayle
Photographer Joe Hancock
Photo Stylists Emily Smoot & Jessica Shinyeda
Hair and Makeup Kathy MacKay
Cover and Interior Designer Julia Boyles
Layout Oceana Garceau
Illustrator Ann Swanson
Production Katherine Jackson

Interweave Press LLC
A division of F+W Media, Inc.
201 East Fourth Street
Loveland, CO 80537
interweave.com

Manufactured in China by RR Donnelley Shenzhen.

Library of Congress Cataloging-in-Publication Data
Budd, Ann, 1956-
Scarf style 2 : innovative to traditional, 25 fresh
designs to knit / Ann Budd.
     pages cm
Follow up to: Scarf style / Pam Allen. — Loveland,
Colo. : Interweave Press, 2004.
Includes index.
ISBN 978-1-59668-781-3 (pbk.)
ISBN 978-1-59668-809-4 (PDF)
1. Knitting—Patterns. 2. Crocheting—Patterns.
3. Scarves. I. Title. II. Title: Scarf style two.
TT825.B8225 2013
746.43'20432—dc23
                                    2012048165

10 9 8 7 6 5 4 3 2 1

In Gratitude

There never would have been a *Scarf Style 2*, or any other books in the ever-expanding *Style* series for that matter, if Pam Allen hadn't written the original *Scarf Style* in 2004. My appreciation for the stage Pam set is endless. And I am indebted to Interweave Press for allowing me to add this latest edition to the series.

Heartfelt thanks go to Kathryn Alexander, Pam Allen, Véronik Avery, Olga Buraya-Kefelian, Nancy Bush, Connie Chang Chinchio, Evelyn A. Clark, Jared Flood, Melissa J. Goodale, Lucinda Guy, Rosemary (Romi) Hill, Mags Kandis, Courtney Kelley, Galina Khmeleva, Nancy Marchant, Laura Nelkin, Deborah Newton, Debbi Stone, Angela Tong, JoLene Treace, Melissa Wehrle, Katya Wilsher, and Alexis Winslow for their contributions of innovative designs that prove that there is no end to exciting cowls, scarves, and shawls.

For their generous contribution of the yarns used in the projects, sincere thanks go to Alpaca with a Twist, Berroco Inc., Blue Sky Alpacas, Blue Moon Fiber Arts, Brooklyn Tweed, Cascade Yarns, Classic Elite Yarns, Dream in Color, Elemental Affects, Fleece Artist, Jojoland International, Kelbourne Woolens, Kathryn Alexander Kits, Knitting Fever Inc., Malabrigo, Misti Alpaca, Quince & Company, St-Denis, Tahki Stacy Charles Inc., Universal Yarns, The Verdant Gryphon, and Westminster Fibers.

For finding and correcting errors in the patterns and charts, Lori Gayle deserves a standing round of applause. Her technical expertise is unsurpassed.

For making this book a visual treat, thanks go to Joe Hancock and his aides Jon Rose and Scott Wallace for superior photography; Emily Smoot and Jessica Smeyda for just-right clothing and accessories; Kathy MacKay for artful hair and makeup; models Amy Elizabeth, Elizabeth Haynes, and Nida Shaheen for wearing everything so well; and Julia Boyles for overseeing it all and for her most excellent book layout and design.

Finally, thanks go to my family of boys—David, Alex, Eric, and Nicholas—for putting up with me and my piles of yarn.

Contents

The Joy of Scarves
(and Shawls and Cowls)

Who knew back in 2004 when Pam Allen wrote the first *Scarf Style* that scarves—and their cousin shawls, cowls, stoles, and wraps—would inspire such creativity among knitters? Instead of being the obligatory first project for beginners, scarves have been elevated to fashion necessities that run the gamut from rustic and casual to sophisticated and elegant. Whereas scarves were once uninventive garter-stitch rectangles, they now include rectangles, tubes, and mobius strips knitted from every direction and in every imaginable stitch pattern.

Like its predecessor *Scarf Style*, *Scarf Style 2* is a book of scarves to knit and a book about knitting scarves. It is a collection of twenty-six patterns from twenty-four knitwear designers, each of whom has instilled unique style into this most basic accessory. From three-dimensional entrelac in Kathryn Alexander's Three-D Entrelac Scarf (page 20), traveling brioche stitches in Nancy Marchant's Brioche Branches (page 46), reversible cables in Pam Allen's Cable-y Cowl (page 54), various knitting directions in Rosemary (Romi) Hill's Winter Garden Wrap (page 90), and tuck stitches in Melissa Wehrle's Shadow Play (page 100), you'll find a wide variety of ideas that will make your fingers itch to cast on. At once relatively small and portable, each project in this book is an individual lesson on inspiration, shaping, knitting direction, and specific techniques—all designed for excellent results.

Knit any of the scarves exactly as shown or use them as springboards for your own creative ideas. All of the design techniques—shape, knitting direction, designing with different stitch patterns, edgings, and embellishments—are explained in the Design Notebook that begins on page 140. By following the guidelines provided, you can make changes to suit your own preferences. To ensure success for even beginning knitters, some patterns are presented as charts as well as row-by-row instructions, and illustrations are provided for most of the techniques used in the projects—just turn to the Glossary of Terms and Techniques that begins on page 160 if you're unsure of how to perform a particular cast-on, bindoff, increase, decrease, or how to join pieces together or add embellishments. The information in this glossary, combined with the easy-to-follow directions and illustrations in the projects and design chapter, will guide you step by step and provide a foundation for exploring your own design ideas. If you want to learn more about techniques, stitch patterns, or shaping, check out the Bibliography on page 174 for an assortment of references.

It's now time to grab yarn and needles and knit a bit of your own scarf style!

Green Cables

DESIGNED BY MELISSA J. GOODALE

For this reversible scarf, **Melissa J. Goodale** worked the cable stitches in a k4, p4 rib pattern so that the knit stitches would stand out on both sides of the fabric. Melissa began the scarf with a tubular cast-on at the neck edge that flows into k2, p2 rib and finished it with a bit of k2, p2 rib and a tubular bind-off at the shoulder edge. Increases worked before the first row of the cable pattern and again after the last row result in a crescent shape that stays put around the neck and shoulders.

FINISHED SIZE
About 62" (157.5 cm) around outer curve and 7¾" (19.5 cm) tall.

YARN
Worsted weight (#4 Medium).

Shown here: Rowan Lima (84% baby alpaca, 8% merino, 8% nylon; 109 yd [100 m]/50 g): #882 Titicaca (green heather), 4 skeins.

NEEDLES
Size U.S. 10½ (6.5 mm): 24" (60 cm) circular (cir).

Adjust needle size if necessary to obtain the correct gauge.

NOTIONS
Cable needle (cn); tapestry needle.

GAUGE
20 sts and 24 rows = 4" (10 cm) in cable patt.

design techniques

Reversible cables, page 148.

Crescent worked from top to bottom, page 147.

Tubular k2, p2 cast-on, page 165.

Lifted increases, see below.

Tubular k2, p2 rib bind-off, page 163.

stitch guide

<u>2/2RC:</u> Sl 2 sts onto cn and hold in back of work, k2, then k2 from cn.

<u>LLI:</u> (left lifted increase) Insert left needle tip into the back of the stitch below the stitch just worked on the right needle, then knit this stitch.

<u>PLLI:</u> (purled left lifted increase) Insert left needle tip into the back of the stitch below the stitch just worked on the right needle, then purl this stitch.

Cable Pattern (multiple of 8 sts + 2)

Rows 1, 3, 4, and 6: K1 through the back loop (k1tbl), *k4, p4; rep from * to last st, sl 1 purlwise with yarn in front (pwise wyf).

Rows 2 and 5: K1tbl, *2/2RC (see Stitch Guide), p4; rep from * to last st, sl 1 pwise wyf.

Rep Rows 1–6 for patt.

notes

○ The scarf shown uses a tubular cast-on and a tubular bind-off (see Glossary), but any elastic cast-on and bind-off methods will also work.

○ The cable pattern is reversible and does not have defined right and wrong sides.

Scarf

Using the k2, p2 tubular method (see Glossary), CO 122 sts. Do not join.

Rows 1–6: K1 through the back loop (k1tbl), *k2, p2; rep from * to last st, sl 1 purlwise with yarn in front (pwise wyf).

Row 7: K1tbl, *[k1, LLI (see Stitch Guide)] 2 times, [p1, PLLI (see Stitch Guide)] 2 times; rep from * to last st, sl 1 pwise wyf—242 sts.

Rows 8–40: Work Rows 1–6 of cable patt (see Stitch Guide) 5 times, then work Rows 1–3 once more.

Row 41: K1tbl, *[k1, LLI] 4 times, [p1, PLLI] 4 times; rep from * to last st, sl 1 pwise wyf—482 sts.

Rows 42–47: K1tbl, *k2, p2; rep from * to last st, sl 1 pwise wyf.

Using the k2, p2 tubular method (see Glossary), BO all sts.

Finishing

Block piece to finished measurements; rib along CO edge will be slightly stretched and rib along BO edge will be almost completely relaxed.

Weave in loose ends.

Queenie

DESIGNED BY LUCINDA GUY

Drawing inspiration from traditional Elizabethan doublet and hose outfits, many of which were elaborately textured and patterned with naturalistic flower and foliate designs, as well as Elizabethan and Moroccan embroidery, **Lucinda Guy** designed this colorfully textural tubular scarf. She turned to the beautiful Moroccan silk designs from a similar period for the hot spice colors. Knitted in the round in two sections that are joined with a three-needle bind-off, this scarf is a warm addition to a winter coat and a comforting layer on a cool spring day.

FINISHED SIZE
About 4½" (11.5 cm) wide and 65" (165 cm) long.

YARN
Sportweight (#2 Fine).

Shown here: Quince and Company Chickadee (100% American wool; 181 yd [166 m]/50 g): #136 nasturtium (A; orange), 3 skeins; #118 chanterelle (B; tan), 2 skeins; #112 pomegranate (red; C), #104 storm (D; gray), #114 Frank's plum (E), and #126 lichen (F; green), 1 skein each.

NEEDLES
Size 3.0 mm (between U.S. size 2 and 3): 16" (40 cm) circular (cir) and set of 5 double-pointed (dpn).

Adjust needle size if necessary to obtain the correct gauge.

NOTIONS
Marker; cable needle (cn); stitch holder; tapestry needle.

GAUGE
28 sts and 34 rnds = 4" (10 cm) in Fair Isle patt worked in rnds, before blocking.

32 sts and 32 rnds = 4" (10 cm) in Fair Isle patt worked in rnds, after blocking.

design techniques

Combined Fair Isle and cable patterns, page 152.

Long tube worked upward from each tail, page 145.

Decorative picot cast-on, page 13.

Three-needle bind-off, page 162.

French knot accents, page 167.

notes

○ The scarf is knitted in two tubular halves, each of which begins with a decorative picot cast-on, then the halves are joined in the center with a three-needle bind-off.

○ To avoid tangling the balls of yarn, make a small bobbin of each color used for the Fair Isle chart.

○ To facilitate the finishing process, weave in the loose ends and work the embroidery as you go; don't leave it to the end.

stitch guide

2/2RC: Sl 2 sts onto cn and hold in back of work, k2, then k2 from cn.

2/2LC: Sl 2 sts onto cn and hold in front of work, k2, then k2 from cn.

1/3RC: Sl 3 sts onto cn and hold in back of work, k1, then p1, k1, p1 from cn.

1/3LC: Sl 1 st onto cn and hold in front of work, k1, p1, k1, then k1 from cn.

Shadow Plait Pattern (multiple of 8 sts)

Rnd 1: *2/2RC (see Stitch Guide), k4; rep from *.

Rnds 2–4: Knit.

Rnd 5: *K4, 2/2LC (see Stitch Guide); rep from *.

Rnds 6–8: Knit.

Rep Rnds 1–8 for patt.

Large Wishbone Pattern (multiple of 12 sts)

Rnd 1: *P2, 1/3 RC, 1/3LC (see Stitch Guide for both cables), p2; rep from *.

Rnds 2, 4, and 6: *P2, k1, [k1, p1] 3 times, k1, p2; rep from *.

Rnds 3, 5, and 7: *P2, k1, [p1, k1] 3 times, k1, p2; rep from *.

Rnd 8: Rep Rnd 2.

Small Wishbone Pattern (multiple of 12 sts)

Rnd 1: *P2, 1/3 RC, 1/3LC, p2; rep from *.

Rnds 2, 4, and 6: *P2, k1, [k1, p1] 3 times, k1, p2; rep from *.

Rnds 3 and 5: *P2, k1, [p1, k1] 3 times, k1, p2; rep from *.

Rnd 7: *P2, k1, p1, k3, p1, k2, p2; rep from *.

Rep Rnds 1–7 for patt.

First Half

With A and 2 dpn, CO 72 decorative picot sts as foll: Use the knitted method (see Glossary) to CO 3 sts, k3tog, slide rem st to opposite tip of dpn, use the knitted method to CO 3 sts (4 sts on needle), k3tog, return the dec'd st to left needle (2 sts on the needle), *CO 3 sts, k3tog, return dec'd st to left needle to add 1 more st; rep from * until there are a total of 72 sts on the needle.

Divide the sts evenly on 4 dpn (18 sts on each needle), place marker (pm), and join for working in rnds. Cutting and joining colors as necessary, work as foll:

Rnds 1–104: Working from chart (see page 15) or Stitch Guide, work Rnds 1–8 of Shadow Plait patt 13 times.

Rnds 105–112: Working from chart or Stitch Guide, work Rnds 1–8 of Large Wishbone patt once.

Rnd 113: *K1 with A, p1 with B; rep from *.

Rnd 114: With B, knit 1 rnd.

Rnds 115–126: Work Rnds 1–12 of Fair Isle chart.

Rnds 127 and 128: With B, knit 2 rnds.

Rnd 129: *K1 with B, p1 with A; rep from *.

Rnds 130 and 131: With A, knit 2 rnds.

Rnds 132–153: Working from chart or Stitch Guide, work Rnds 1–7 of Small Wishbone patt 3 times, then work Rnd 1 once more.

Rnd 154: *K1 with A, p1 with B; rep from *.

Rnd 155: With B, knit 1 rnd.

Rnds 156–160: Rnds 1–5 of Peerie chart, working single purl sts in Rnds 2 and 4 of chart as shown.

Rnds 161 and 162: With B, knit 2 rnds.

Rnds 163–196: Work Rnds 1–34 of Fair Isle chart.

Rnds 197 and 198: With B, knit 2 rnds.

Rnd 199: *K1 with B, p1 with A; rep from *.

Rnds 200 and 201: With A, knit 2 rnds.

Rnds 202–209: Work Rnds 1–8 of Large Wishbone patt.

Rnd 210: *K1 with A, p1 with B; rep from *.

Rnd 211: With B, knit 1 rnd.

Rnds 212–223: Work Rnds 1–12 of Fair Isle chart.

Rnds 224 and 225: With B, knit 2 rnds.

Rnd 226: *K1 with B, p1 with A; rep from *.

Rnds 227 and 228: With A, knit 2 rnds.

Rnds 229–236: Work Rnds 1–8 of Large Wishbone patt.

Rnds 281 and 282: With A, knit 2 rnds.

Rnds 283–290: Work Rnds 1–8 of Large Wishbone patt.

Place sts on holder.

Second Half

Work picot CO and Rnds 1–282 as for first half, omitting the final Large Wishbone patt from Rnds 283–290. Place sts on holder.

Finishing

With F threaded on a tapestry needle, work French knots (see Glossary) as indicated in Rnds 3, 14, and 25 of Fair Isle chart if you have not already done so.

Turn one scarf half inside out, and slip the other half inside it so that the right sides are touching and the wrong sides are visible. With A, use the three-needle method (see Glossary) to join the two halves of the scarf. Turn entire scarf right side out.

Flatten the scarf, making sure the fold lines at each side are aligned with the same stitch column all along the scarf, and use A to sew ends of tube closed just above the picot CO.

Weave in loose ends.

Wash very carefully in warm soapy water and rinse well. Gently squeeze out excess moisture by rolling in a towel. Pull into shape and lay flat to dry away from direct heat or sun.

Rnd 237: *K1 with A, p1 with B; rep from *.

Rnd 238: With B, knit 1 rnd.

Rnds 239–250: Knit 1 rnd with A, then work Rnds 13–23 of Fair Isle chart.

Rnds 251 and 252: With B, knit 2 rnds.

Rnd 253: *K1 with B, p1 with A; rep from *.

Rnds 254 and 255: With A, knit 2 rnds.

Rnds 256–263: Work Rnds 1–8 of Large Wishbone patt.

Rnd 264: *K1 with A, p1 with B; rep from *.

Rnd 265: With B, knit 1 rnd.

Rnds 266–277: Work Rnds 1–12 of Fair Isle chart.

Rnds 278 and 279: With B, knit 2 rnds.

Rnd 280: *K1 with B, p1 with A; rep from *.

Fair Isle

33
31
29
27
25
23
21
19
17
15
13
11
9
7
5
3
1

12-st repeat

Peerie

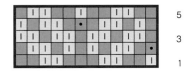

5
3
1

12-st repeat

Shadow Plait

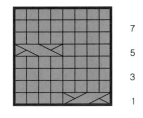

7
5
3
1

8-st repeat

Small Wishbone

7
5
3
1

12-st repeat

Large Wishbone

7
5
3
1

12-st repeat

A, knit

· A, purl

| B, knit

× C, knit

+ D, knit

E, knit

knit with B, French knot with F

pattern repeat

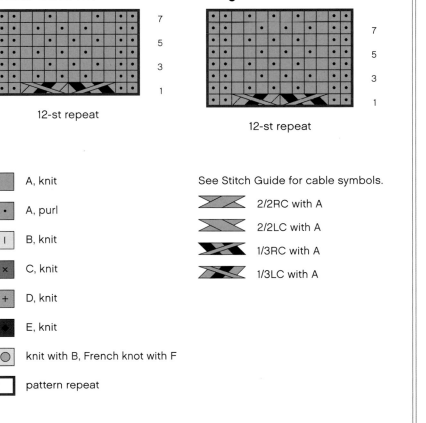

See Stitch Guide for cable symbols.

2/2RC with A

2/2LC with A

1/3RC with A

1/3LC with A

Nordic Cowl

DESIGNED BY MAGS KANDIS

Armed with chunky baby alpaca, **Mags Kandis** designed this cowl for the ultimate luxury around an exposed neck. Mags chose simple Fair Isle patterns that she worked in charcoal and ecru, then she added contrasting French knot accents and a crocheted edging at the top for a splash of unexpected color. To prevent the extremely drapey fabric from flopping open at the top of the cowl and exposing too much of the wrong side of the knitting, she added contrasting braided ties near the upper edge that help snug the tube in place.

FINISHED SIZE

About 25" (63.5 cm) in circumference and 11" (28 cm) tall, including crochet frill.

YARN

Chunky weight (#5 Bulky).

Shown here: Cascade Yarns Baby Alpaca Chunky (100% baby alpaca; 108 yd [99 m]/100 g): #570 charcoal (A), #565 ecru (B), and #591 mustard (C), 1 skein each.

Note: Cowl shown used almost all of color A with only about 8 yards (7.3 meters) left over.

NEEDLES

Sizes U.S. 8 and 10 (5 and 6 mm): one 24" (60 cm) circular (cir) needle each size.

Adjust needle size if necessary to obtain the correct gauge.

NOTIONS

Marker (m); tapestry needle; size H/8 (5 mm) crochet hook.

GAUGE

14 sts and 16 rnds = 4" (10 cm) in charted pattern on larger needle.

design techniques

Fair Isle patterns, page 151.

Short tube worked from bottom up, page 145.

Garter-stitch edging, page 154.

Crochet frill, page 155.

French knot accents, page 167.

Braided ties, page 19.

Cowl

With A and smaller cir needle, CO 88 sts. Place marker (pm) and join for working in rnds, being careful not to twist sts.

[Knit 1 rnd, purl 1 rnd] 2 times—2 garter ridges completed; piece measures about ¾" (2 cm).

Change to larger cir needle.

Work Rnds 1–36 of Nordic chart, working 8-st patt rep 11 times around—piece measures about 9¾" (25 cm) from CO.

Change to smaller cir needle and A.

[Knit 1 rnd, purl 1 rnd] 2 times—2 garter ridges completed; piece measures about 10½" (26.5 cm) from CO.

BO all sts knitwise.

Finishing

Weave in loose ends.

Block lightly to measurements, if necessary.

Crochet Frill

Note: *See Glossary for crochet instructions.*

With C, crochet hook, and RS facing, join yarn by working a sl st into first BO st at upper edge of cowl.

Frill rnd: *Ch 7, sl st into next BO st; rep from * to end.

Cut yarn, fasten off last st, and secure tail on WS.

Embroidery

With C threaded on a tapestry needle, work 4-wrap French knots (see Glossary) at positions shown in Rnd 27 of chart.

Ties

Mark positions for two ties in Rnd 35 of chart; the first aligned with the 17th st of the rnd and the second aligned with the 73rd st of the rnd.

Cut six strands of C, each 30" (76 cm) long.

Thread three strands on a tapestry needle, insert the needle from front to back next to one of the marked sts, go under the marked st, and then bring the needle out from back to front on the other side of the same st. Pull the six ends of the strands even, divide them into three groups of two each, and work a braid about 8" (20.5 cm) long. Tie the ends in an overhand knot and trim about 1" (2.5 cm) below the knot.

Repeat for the second tie using the rem three strands of C.

Nordic

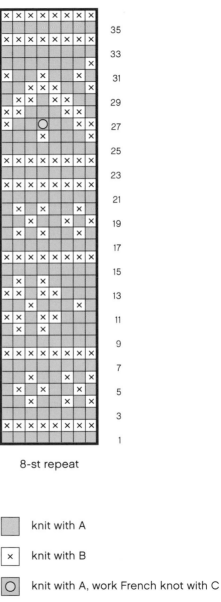

8-st repeat

	knit with A
×	knit with B
O	knit with A, work French knot with C
	pattern repeat

Three-D Entrelac Scarf

DESIGNED BY
KATHRYN
ALEXANDER

For this riotously colorful scarf, **Kathryn Alexander** set out to make a relatively simple tubular scarf using her signature entrelac process. Knowing that alternating right- and left-leaning tiers in regular entrelac produces a flat fabric, Kathryn worked two successive tiers in the same direction in order to create the bold three-dimensional effect you see here. Although the knitting is simple and repetitive, Kathryn incorporated twenty-five of her hand-dyed colors and added striped I-cord fringe for a look that's distinctly Kathryn. Mix and match colors to suit your own style.

FINISHED SIZE

About 6" (15 cm) wide (flattened) and 64" (162.5 cm) long, excluding fringe.

YARN

Sportweight (#2 Fine).

Shown here: Kathryn Alexander's hand-dyed woolen singles (100% wool; 60 yd [55 m]/15 g): 1 skein each in 25 colors: royal blue, smoky purple, fuchsia, forest green, coral, yellow-green, gray rose, spruce green, brown, golden mustard, gray mint, rose haze, faded denim, violet, rusty orange, mossy green, magenta, gray violet, soft mint, gray, light orange rust, green gold, soft pink, bright pink, and purple rose.

Note: The yarn for this scarf is available as a kit from kathrynalexander.net.

NEEDLES

Size U.S. 4 (3.5 mm): 16" (40 cm) circular (cir) and set of 2 double-pointed (dpn).

Adjust needle size if necessary to obtain the correct gauge.

NOTIONS

Stitch holders; spare 16" (40 cm) cir needle same size or smaller than main needle; tapestry needle.

GAUGE

12 sts and 16 rows = 2" (5 cm) in St st.

One entrelac rectangle (14 sts wide and 27 rows high) measures about 2¼" (5.5 cm) wide and 3¼" (8.5 cm) high.

design techniques

Three-dimensional multicolored entrelac, page 152.

Long tube worked upward from each tail, page 145.

Three-needle bind-off, page 162.

I-cord fringe, page 26.

color order

<u>Note</u>: This list contains 21 of the 25 colors used in the project; the remaining 4 colors are used at the ends of the scarf halves according to the directions.

- royal blue (base triangles)
- smoky purple
- fuchsia
- forest green
- coral
- yellow-green
- gray rose
- spruce green
- brown
- golden mustard
- gray mint
- rose haze
- faded denim
- violet
- rusty orange
- mossy green
- magenta
- gray violet
- soft mint
- gray
- light orange rust

notes

- The scarf is made in two halves, each worked from the cast-on edge toward the center, then the double I-cord fringe is applied during finishing.

- Each set of three-dimensional peaks consists of two tiers of entrelac rectangles, either both right-leaning tiers or both left-leaning tiers.

- The first half of the scarf begins with left-leaning base triangles and ends with a set of right-leaning peaks. The second half begins with right-leaning base triangles and ends with a set of left-leaning peaks. Because the last set of peaks in each half is a mirror image of the other, it is possible to fit the two halves together so the pieces can be joined invisibly using a three-needle bind-off.

- To save time and ensure the surface is neat and even, weave in ends as you work.

First Half

With royal blue and cir needle, CO 56 sts. Place marker (pm) and join for working in rnds, being careful not to twist sts.

Knit 1 rnd, then purl 1 rnd, remove m.

Left-Leaning Base Triangles

With RS still facing, cont as foll:

Row 1: (RS) K2, turn work.

Row 2: (WS) P2, turn.

Rows 3 and 4: K3, turn, p3, turn.

Rows 5 and 6: K4, turn, p4, turn.

Rows 7 and 8: K5, turn, p5, turn.

Rows 9 and 10: K6, turn, p6, turn.

Rows 11 and 12: K7, turn, p7, turn.

Rows 13 and 14: K8, turn, p8, turn.

Rows 15 and 16: K9, turn, p9, turn.

Rows 17 and 18: K10, turn, p10, turn.

Rows 19 and 20: K11, turn, p11, turn.

Rows 21 and 22: K12, turn, p12, turn.

Rows 23 and 24: K13, turn, p13, turn.

Row 25: (RS) K14; do not turn.

*With RS still facing work Row 1 again, then work Rows 2–25; rep from * 2 more times—four 14-st left-leaning base triangles completed; all CO sts have been worked.

Cut yarn.

Right-Leaning Peaks

Each right-leaning peak consists of two tiers of right-leaning rectangles.

First tier of right-leaning rectangles

Join next color (see Color Order) to the "peak" of any triangle or rectangle unit from the previous tier.

Row 1: With WS facing, pick up and purl (see Glossary) 13 sts evenly spaced along selvedge from "peak" to "valley" between units, then purl 1 st from next group of 14 live sts on left needle, turn work—14 sts for this rectangle.

Even-numbered Rows 2–26: (RS) K14, turn.

Odd-numbered Rows 3–25: (WS) P13, p2tog (last rectangle st tog with next live st after it) to join 1 st of adjacent group, turn.

Row 27: (WS) Rep Row 3; do not turn—14 sts for this rectangle; all live sts of adjacent group have been joined.

*With WS still facing work Row 1 again, then work Rows 2–27; rep from * 2 more times—four 14-st right-leaning rectangles completed; no live sts rem from previous tier.

Cut yarn.

Second tier of right-leaning rectangles

Join next color in the "valley" between any two units of the previous tier.

Row 1: With WS facing, pick up and purl 13 sts evenly spaced along selvedge from "valley" to "peak" between units, then purl 1 st from next group of 14 live sts on left needle, turn work—14 sts for this rectangle.

Even-numbered Rows 2–26: (RS) K14, turn.

Odd-numbered Rows 3–25: (WS) P13, p2tog (last rectangle st tog with next live st after it) to join 1 st of adjacent group, turn.

Row 27: (WS) Rep Row 3; do not turn—14 sts for this rectangle; all live sts of adjacent group have been joined.

*With WS still facing work Row 1 again, then work Rows 2–27; rep from * 2 more times—four 14-st right-leaning rectangles completed; no live sts rem from previous tier.

Cut yarn.

The first and second tier together complete one set of right-leaning peaks.

Left-Leaning Peaks

Each left-leaning peak consists of two tiers of left-leaning rectangles.

First tier of left-leaning rectangles

Join next color to the "peak" of any triangle or rectangle unit from the previous tier.

Row 1: With RS facing, pick up and knit 13 sts evenly spaced along selvedge from "peak" to "valley" between units, then knit 1 st from next group of 14 sts on left needle, turn work—14 sts for this rectangle.

Even-numbered Rows 2–26: (WS) P14, turn.

Odd-numbered Rows 3–25: (RS) K13, ssk (last rectangle st tog with next live st after it) to join 1 st of adjacent group.

Row 27: Rep Row 3; do not turn—14 sts for this rectangle; all live sts of adjacent group have been joined.

*With RS still facing, work Row 1 again, then work Rows 2–27; rep from * two more times—four 14-st left-leaning rectangles completed; no live sts rem from previous tier.

Cut yarn.

Second tier of left-leaning rectangles

Join next color in the "valley" between any two units of the previous tier.

Row 1: With RS facing, pick up and knit 13 sts evenly spaced along selvedge from "valley" to "peak" between units, then knit 1 st from next group of 14 sts on left needle, turn work—14 sts for this rectangle.

Even-numbered Rows 2–26: (WS) P14, turn.

Odd-numbered Rows 3–25: (RS) K13, ssk (last rectangle st tog with next live st after it) to join 1 st of adjacent group.

Row 27: Rep Row 3; do not turn—14 sts for this rectangle; all live sts of adjacent group have been joined.

*With RS still facing, work Row 1 again, then work Rows 2–27; rep from * two more times—four 14-st left-leaning rectangles completed; no live sts rem from previous tier.

Cut yarn.

The first and second tier together complete one set of left-leaning peaks.

Next 8 Peaks

Cont to change colors for each tier according to the Color Order, [work a set of right-leaning peaks, then work a set of left-leaning peaks] 4 more times, ending with light orange rust—10 sets of peaks total (5 each right- and left-leaning) and one tier of base triangles; 56 sts in four groups of 14 sts each. Leave sts on needle.

Last Peak

Work one more right-leaning peak using green gold for the first tier of rectangles and soft pink for the second tier—11 sets of peaks total (6 right-leaning and 5 left-leaning) and one tier of base triangles; 56 sts in four groups of 14 sts each. Place sts on holder.

Second Half

With royal blue and cir needle, CO 56 sts. Pm and join for working in rnds, being careful not to twist sts.

Knit 1 rnd, then purl 1 rnd, remove m.

Right-Leaning Base Triangles

Turn work so WS is facing, and cont as foll:

Row 1: (WS) P2, turn work.

Row 2: (RS) K2, turn.

Rows 3 and 4: P3, turn, k3, turn.

Rows 5 and 6: P4, turn, k4, turn.

Rows 7 and 8: P5, turn, k5, turn.

Rows 9 and 10: P6, turn, k6, turn.

Rows 11 and 12: P7, turn, k7, turn.

Rows 13 and 14: P8, turn, k8, turn.

Rows 15 and 16: P9, turn, k9, turn.

Rows 17 and 18: P10, turn, k10, turn.

Rows 19 and 20: P11, turn, k11, turn.

Rows 21 and 22: P12, turn, k12, turn.

Rows 23 and 24: P13, turn, k13, turn.

Row 25: (WS) P14; do not turn.

*With WS still facing work Row 1 again, then work Rows 2–25; rep from * 2 more times—four 14-st right-leaning base triangles completed; all CO sts have been worked.

Cut yarn.

Next 10 Peaks

Cont to change colors for each tier according to the Color Order and working according to directions in first half, [work a set of left-leaning peaks, then work a set of right-leaning peaks] 5 times, ending with light orange rust—10 sets of peaks (5 each left- and right-leaning) and one tier of base triangles; 56 sts in four groups of 14 sts each. Leave sts on needle.

Last Peak

Work one more left-leaning peak using purple rose for the first tier of rectangles and bright pink for the second tier—11 sets of peaks total (6 left-leaning and 5 right-leaning) and one tier of base triangles; 56 sts in four groups of 14 sts each. Leave sts on needle.

Finishing

Note: *Each 14-stitch group of live stitches in one half of the scarf will be joined to the selvedge of a rectangle in the other half. To make this possible, each live stitch is worked together with a stitch picked up from the selvedge of a corresponding rectangle.*

Place live sts from first half of scarf on spare cir needle. Turn one half inside out and slip the other half inside it so the right sides are touching and the wrong sides of each half are visible on the inside and outside of the tube. Adjust the pieces as necessary to bring a 14-st group of live sts from one half of the scarf together and parallel with the selvedge of a rectangle in the other half, with the needle holding the live stitches in front.

With matching color and an empty dpn, insert the right needle into the first st on the front needle, then into the selvedge of the rectangle on the back needle to pick up and knit 1 st, wrap yarn around needle again as if to knit, and draw the loop through both sts to work them tog—1 st on right needle.

Picking up evenly-spaced sts from the rectangle on the back needle, *insert the right needle into the next st on front needle, then into the selvedge of the rectangle on the back needle to pick up and knit 1 st, work both sts tog (2 sts on right needle), pass first st over the second to BO 1 st; rep from * to join all live sts in this 14-st group to the rectangle selvedge on the back needle.

Cont working around the scarf in this manner until all 14-st groups of live sts on the front needle have been joined. Turn piece so inside of tube is facing, and join the rem 14-st groups of live sts to the rem rectangle selvedges in the same manner.

Weave in ends if you have not already done so. Turn scarf right side out.

Double I-Cord Checkerboard Fringe

Note: *Each fringe consists of a pair of 3-st, two-color I-cords, with the fringe colors used randomly. Three evenly-spaced fringes are applied to the cast-on edge of each base triangle.*

With the color of your choice, dpn, and RS facing, pick up and knit 3 sts along the CO edge of a royal blue triangle, then, with a second color, pick up and knit 3 more sts— 6 sts total; 3 sts in each color.

Row 1: With RS facing, slide sts to right tip of needle, and, working each st with its matching color, bring first color tightly across back of work, k3, bring second color tightly across back of work, k3.

Row 2: Rep Row 1.

Row 3: With RS facing, slide sts to right tip of needle. Working each st using the opposite color, bring first color tightly across back of work and k3, then bring second color tightly across back of work and k3. (Note: Exchanging the colors will tack the I-cords together at each color change row.)

Rows 4 and 5: Working each st with its matching color, rep Row 1.

Rep Rows 3–5 eleven more times—one 2-row block and twelve 3-row blocks completed.

Work Row 3 again to change colors one last time, then rep Row 1 every row 18 times—18 unjoined rows at end of fringe. BO each unjoined I-cord using its matching color. Tie an overhand knot in the end of each I-cord, cut yarn, thread tail on a tapestry needle, and conceal the tail in the knot. Weave in starting tails.

Choosing pairs of colors at random, make 11 more fringes around the same end of the scarf so that there are 3 evenly-spaced double I-cords in each of the 4 royal blue base triangles. For the other end of the scarf, work 12 double I-cords in the same manner, working 3 double I-cords in each royal blue base triangle.

Cottage Scarf

DESIGNED BY JARED FLOOD

Jared Flood tries to knit a classic cabled scarf every winter. For the masculine design shown here, he decided to include a few subtle details for a slightly more contemporary take on traditional Aran patterning—a k2, p2 tubular cast-on and bind-off, a deep ribbed hem, and a slim I-cord edging. He also combined one strand each of gray and brown yarn to create a thick, but far from stiff, scarf with a tweedy look. To make the scarf distinctly your own, choose colors to match your wardrobe.

FINISHED SIZE

About 61 (75½, 90)" (155 [192, 228.5] cm) long and 6½" (16.5 cm) wide, measured relaxed after blocking.

Scarf shown measures 75½" (192 cm).

YARN

Worsted weight (#4 Medium) or two strands of fingering weight (#1 Super Fine) held together.

Shown here: Brooklyn Tweed Loft (100% U.S. Targhee-Columbia wool; 275 yd [251 m]/50 g); soot (gray) and truffle hunt (brown), 2 (2, 3) skeins each.

NEEDLES

Ribbing: size U.S. 7 (4.5 mm).

Body: size U.S. 8 (5 mm).

Adjust needle size if necessary to obtain the correct gauge.

NOTIONS

Two cable needles (cn); tapestry needle.

GAUGE

18 sts and 28 rows = 4" (10 cm) in St st on larger needles using double strand of yarn (see Notes), after blocking.

41 sts and 96 rows of Main Repeat chart measure 6½" (16.5 cm) wide and 14½" (37 cm) high on larger needles using double strand of yarn, relaxed after blocking.

design techniques

Flat rectangle worked from tail to tail, page 144.

Combined cable patterns, page 148.

Tubular k2, p2 cast-on, page 165.

Ribbed edging at each end, page 154.

I-cord edging along sides worked simultaneously with body, at right.

Tubular k2, p2 rib bind-off, page 163.

stitch guide

LT: Sl 1 st onto cn and hold in front of work, k1, then k1 from cn.

Ribbing with I-cord Edges
(multiple of 4 sts + 2)

Row 1: (RS) *K2, p2; rep from * to last 2 sts, sl 2 purlwise with yarn in front (pwise wyf).

Row 2: (WS) K4, *p2, k2; rep from * to last 2 sts, sl 2 pwise wyf.

Rep Rows 1 and 2 for patt.

notes

○ This project is worked using one strand of each fingering-weight color held together throughout for the equivalent of a worsted-weight yarn.

○ A built-in 2-stitch I-cord is worked along each selvedge. Instructions for working the edge are given during the first few rows, as well as shown on the chart. Work the first and last 2 stitches of each row in 2-stitch I-cord from start to finish.

○ To lengthen or shorten the scarf, work the Main Repeat chart more or fewer times; each repeat will add or subtract about 14½" (37 cm) of length. Keep in mind that yarn requirements will be affected.

Scarf

With one strand of each color held tog and smaller needles, use the k2, p2 tubular method (see Glossary) to CO 38 sts.

Set-up Row 1: (RS) *K2, p2; rep from * to last 2 sts, sl 2 purlwise with yarn in front (pwise wyf).

Set-up Row 2: (WS) LT (see Stitch Guide), *k2, p2; rep from * to last 4 sts, k2, sl 2 pwise wyf.

Change to working ribbing with I-cord edges (see Stitch Guide) and work until piece measures 3" (7.5 cm) from CO, ending with a RS row.

Next row: (WS) Work set-up row of Beginning chart (see page 30), inc as shown on chart—41 sts.

Change to larger needles.

Maintaining I-cord edging as established (knit the first 2 sts and slip the last 2 sts pwise wyf every row), work Rows 1–32 of Beginning chart. Change to Main Repeat chart, and work Rows 1–96 of chart 3 (4, 5) times. Change to Ending chart and work Rows 1–39, ending with a RS row.

Change to smaller needles.

Next row: (WS) Work Row 40 of Ending chart, dec as shown on chart—38 sts rem.

Work ribbing with I-cord edges until piece measures 3" (7.5 cm) from Row 40 of last chart (i.e., work the same number of ribbing rows as at the beginning of the scarf), ending with a WS row. Using the tubular k2, p2 method (see Glossary), BO all sts.

Beginning

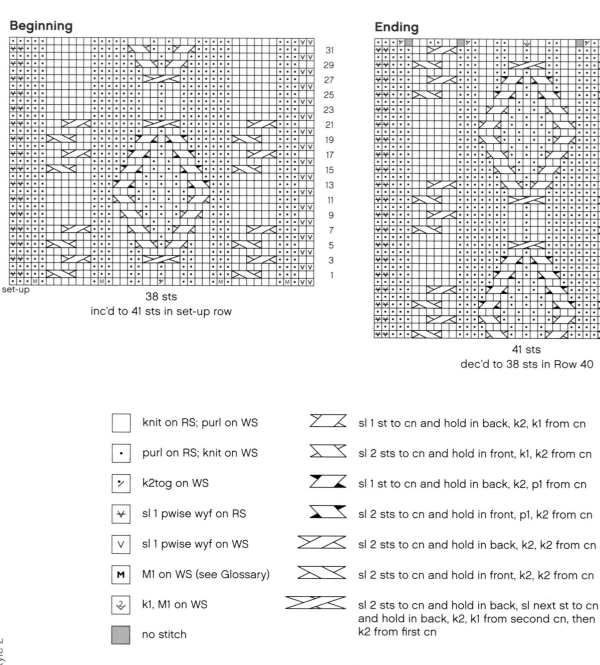

set-up

38 sts
inc'd to 41 sts in set-up row

Ending

41 sts
dec'd to 38 sts in Row 40

☐ knit on RS; purl on WS	⊐⊏ sl 1 st to cn and hold in back, k2, k1 from cn
• purl on RS; knit on WS	⊏⊐ sl 2 sts to cn and hold in front, k1, k2 from cn
⟩ k2tog on WS	⊐◣ sl 1 st to cn and hold in back, k2, p1 from cn
⩔ sl 1 pwise wyf on RS	◢⊐ sl 2 sts to cn and hold in front, p1, k2 from cn
v sl 1 pwise wyf on WS	⊐⊏ sl 2 sts to cn and hold in back, k2, k2 from cn
M M1 on WS (see Glossary)	⊏⊐ sl 2 sts to cn and hold in front, k2, k2 from cn
⟱ k1, M1 on WS	⊐⊏ sl 2 sts to cn and hold in back, sl next st to cn and hold in back, k2, k1 from second cn, then k2 from first cn
▨ no stitch	

Main Repeat

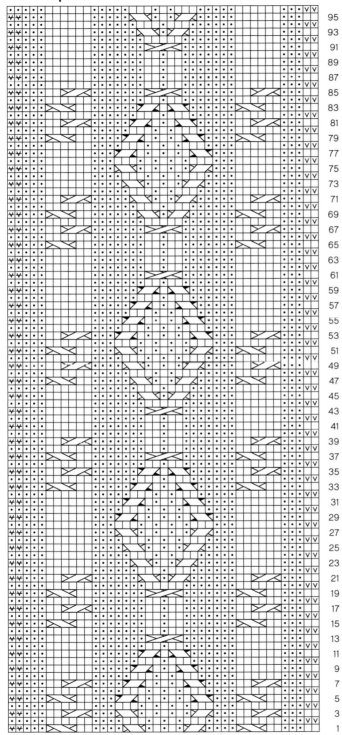

95
93
91
89
87
85
83
81
79
77
75
73
71
69
67
65
63
61
59
57
55
53
51
49
47
45
43
41
39
37
35
33
31
29
27
25
23
21
19
17
15
13
11
9
7
5
3
1

41 sts

Finishing

Wet-block scarf to finished measurements using blocking wires and stretching the ribbing at each end to the same width as the scarf body to prevent it from drawing in too much with wear. Allow to air-dry completely before removing blocking wires.

Weave in loose ends invisibly on WS of fabric.

Passing Through Shawl

DESIGNED BY
DEBBI STONE

Attracted to the shape and versatility of classic working shawls, **Debbi Stone** designed this piece to be large enough to wrap around the shoulders and tie in the back to create a sort of vest to allow full arm movement. Worked from the neck down, Debbi placed a lace panel along the center and a decorative cable edging along the bottom. The cable edging "passes" along the hem and the cables pass "through" the lace as they travel up the back of the shawl— hence, the name Passing Through.

FINISHED SIZE

About 73" (185.5 cm) wide across top edge and 19" (48.5 cm) long from center of top edge to bottom point, after blocking.

YARN

Worsted weight (#4 Medium).

Shown here: Blue Moon Fiber Arts Woobu (60% merino, 40% bamboo; 620 yd [567 m]/8 oz [226 g]): spinel (denim blue), 1 skein.

NEEDLES

Size U.S. 8 (5 mm): 32" (80 cm) circular (cir).

Adjust needle size if necessary to obtain the correct gauge.

NOTIONS

Markers (m); cable needle (cn); tapestry needle.

GAUGE

16 sts and 29 rows = 4" (10 cm) in St st, after blocking.

29 sts of lace panel patt measure 7¾" (19.5 cm) wide, after blocking.

10 sts of border patt measure about 2¼" (5.5 cm) at widest point, after blocking.

design techniques

Combined cable and lace patterns, page 152.

Triangle worked from top to bottom and shaped with increases, page 147.

Yarnover increases, page 168.

Narrow band of stockinette forms foundation for central lace pattern, page 35.

Cable/lace border joined to long edge as it is worked, pages 154–155.

stitch guide

CDD: (centered double decrease) Sl 2 sts tog as if to k2tog, k1, p2sso—2 sts dec'd.

3/3RC: Sl 3 sts onto cn and hold in back of work, k3, then k3 from cn.

Lace Panel (worked over 29 sts)

Row 1: (RS) K1, [yo, ssk, k1, k2tog, yo, k6] 2 times, yo, ssk, k1, k2tog, yo, k1.

Even-numbered Rows 2–10: (WS) K1, p27, k1.

Row 3: K2, [yo, CDD (see above), yo, k1, 3/3RC (see above), k1] 2 times, yo, CDD, yo, k2.

Row 5: Rep Row 1.

Row 7: K2, [yo, CDD, yo, k8] 2 times, yo, CDD, yo, k2.

Row 9: K1, [yo, ssk, k1, k2tog, yo, 3/3RC] 2 times, yo, ssk, k1, k2tog, yo, k1.

Row 11: Rep Row 7.

Row 12: Rep Row 2.

Rep Rows 1–12 for patt.

Border (worked over 10 sts)

Join the border to the shawl body by working the last border st of every RS row tog with the live shawl body st after it as foll:

Row 1: (RS) Sl 1 pwise wyf, p1, k6, p1, p2tog (last border st and next shawl st)—1 shawl st joined.

Even-numbered Rows 2–22: K2, p6, k2.

Row 3: Sl 1 pwise wyf, p1, 3/3RC, p1, p2tog (last border st and next shawl st)—1 shawl st joined.

Row 5: Sl 1 pwise wyf, p1, k6, p1, p2tog (last border st and next shawl st)—1 shawl st joined.

Row 7: Sl 1 pwise wyf, p1, k1, yo, k2tog, k3, p1, p2tog (last border st and next shawl st)—1 shawl st joined.

Row 9: Sl 1 pwise wyf, p1, ssk, yo, k4, p1, p2tog (last border st and next shawl st)—1 shawl st joined.

Row 11: Rep Row 7—1 shawl st joined.

Row 13: Rep Row 1—1 shawl st joined.

Row 15: Rep Row 3—1 shawl st joined.

Row 17: Rep Row 1—1 shawl st joined.

Row 19: Sl 1 pwise wyf, p1, k3, ssk, yo, k1, p1, p2tog—1 shawl st joined.

Row 21: Sl 1 pwise wyf, p1, k4, yo, k2tog, p1, p2tog—1 shawl st joined.

Row 23: Rep Row 19—1 shawl st joined.

Row 24: Rep Row 2.

Rep Rows 1–24 for patt—12 shawl body sts joined for every 24 border rows.

note

○ The gauge for this project is deliberately worked slightly looser than normal for worsted-weight yarn to create a softly draping fabric.

Shawl

CO 3 sts. Do not join.

Knit 58 rows for center of top edge—29 garter ridges completed.

Rotate piece 90 degrees so that needle with live sts is to the right and selvedge of piece is across the top. With same side still facing, pick up and knit 29 sts evenly spaced (about 1 st between each pair of garter ridges) along selvedge edge—32 sts. With same side still facing, rotate piece 90 degrees again, then pick up and knit 1 st from each of the 3 CO sts—35 sts total.

Set-up Row 1: (RS) Sl 1 purlwise with yarn in front (pwise wyf), k2, place marker (pm), yo, pm, k29, pm, yo, pm, k3—37 sts.

Set-up Row 2: Sl 1 pwise wyf, k2, slip marker (sl m), yo, purl to m before last 3 sts, yo, sl m, k3—39 sts total; 3 edge sts at each side; 29 sts in center section; 2 sts each in sections inside edge sts.

Body

Working Lace Panel patt from chart (see page 37) or Stitch Guide, work as foll:

Row 1: (RS) Sl 1 pwise wyf, k2, sl m, yo, knit to next m, yo, sl m, work Row 1 of Lace Panel over center 29 sts, sl m, yo, knit to next m, yo, sl m, k3—4 sts inc'd total; 2 sts inc'd in each section inside edge sts.

Rows 2, 4, 6, 8, and 10: (WS) Sl 1 pwise wyf, k2, sl m, yo, purl to m, sl m, work 29 sts of lace panel as established, sl m, purl to next m, yo, sl m, k3—2 sts inc'd each row; 1 st inc'd in each section inside edge sts.

Rows 3, 5, 7, 9, and 11: Sl 1 pwise wyf, k2, sl m, yo, knit to m, yo, sl m, work 29 sts lace panel as established, sl m, yo, knit to next m, yo, sl m, k3—4 sts inc'd in each row; 2 sts inc'd in each section inside edge sts.

Row 12: Rep Row 2—2 sts inc'd total; 1 st inc'd in each section inside edge sts; 36 sts total inc'd in Rows 1–12; 18 sts total inc'd in each St st section inside edge sts.

Cont in established patt, rep Rows 1–12 six more times—291 sts total; 3 edge sts at each side; 29 sts in center section; 128 sts in each St st section inside edge sts.

Work Rows 1–11 once more, ending with a RS row—325 sts total; 3 edge sts at each side; 29 sts in center section; 145 sts in each St st section inside edge sts.

Next row: (WS) Sl 1 pwise wyf, knit to end, removing markers as you come to them, then use the knitted method (see Glossary) to CO 10 sts for border—325 shawl sts; 10 new CO sts.

Border

Working border patt from chart or Stitch Guide, work Rows 1–12 of border patt 27 times, then work Row 1 once more—10 border sts rem; all shawl body sts have been joined.

Next row: (WS) [P2tog] 5 times—5 sts rem.

Next row: (RS) Sl 1 pwise wyf, k2, ssk—4 sts rem.

BO all sts pwise.

Finishing

Weave in loose ends. Block to measurements.

Lace Panel

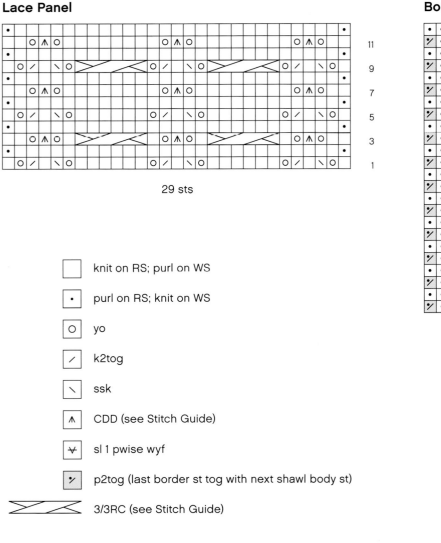

29 sts

Border

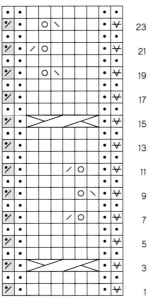

10 sts

	knit on RS; purl on WS
•	purl on RS; knit on WS
O	yo
/	k2tog
\	ssk
∧	CDD (see Stitch Guide)
⩔	sl 1 pwise wyf
⁄/	p2tog (last border st tog with next shawl body st)
	3/3RC (see Stitch Guide)

Checkered Cowl

DESIGNED BY OLGA BURAYA-KEFELIAN

Olga Buraya-Kefelian's fascination with linear texture provided the main inspiration for the intersecting welts and dropped stitches that give a "checkerboard" look to this unusual cowl. She added colored stripes for more visual complexity and interest. Worked as a flat rectangle, the piece begins with a provisional cast-on that is joined to the last row of knitting with the Kitchener stitch to form a seamless loop. To minimize the number of ends to weave in, the unused color is carried along the selvedge and twisted around the working yarn until it is needed again.

FINISHED SIZE
About 48" (122 cm) in circumference and 7¾" (19.5 cm) wide.

YARN
Fingering weight (#1 Super Fine).

Shown here: Malabrigo Sock (100% superwash merino; (440 yd [402 m]/100 g): #811 eggplant (A) and #802 terracotta (B), 1 skein each.

NEEDLES
Size U.S. 4 (3.5 mm).

Adjust needle size if necessary to obtain the correct gauge.

NOTIONS
About 2 yd (2 m) smooth waste yarn in weight similar to main yarn; tapestry needle.

GAUGE
27½ sts and 42½ rows = 4" (10 cm) in dropped st patt, after dropping sts.

design techniques

Reversible texture and color pattern, page 153.

Flat rectangle joined into a tube, page 146.

Provisional cast-on, page 164.

Kitchener stitch, page 169.

note

○ Instead of cutting the yarn at each color change, carry the unused color up along the selvedge to where it is needed again, twisting the unused strand neatly with the working color to avoid leaving floats.

Rep these 12 rows 38 more times, then work Rows 1–10 once more—478 rows total; piece measures about 45" (114.5 cm) from CO.

Next row: (RS) With B, [p5, drop next st and let it ravel all the way to CO edge] 8 times, p5.

Cut B, leaving a 24" (61 cm) tail.

Cowl

With smooth waste yarn and using a provisional method (see Glossary), CO 53 sts.

Change to A and cont as foll:

Row 1: (RS) Knit.

Row 2: (WS) Purl.

Rows 3–6: Rep Rows 1 and 2 two more times.

Change to B and cont as foll:

Rows 7 and 8: Knit.

Row 9: Purl.

Row 10: Knit.

Rows 11 and 12: Purl.

Finishing

Carefully remove waste yarn from provisional CO and place exposed sts on empty needle. Fold the piece in half with needles parallel and so that RS face tog and WS face out, being careful not to twist the piece. Thread color B tail on a tapestry needle and use the Kitchener st (see Glossary) to graft the live sts tog with exposed sts from provisional CO, taking care to match the distance between the sts at the gaps formed by dropped sts.

Soak in warm water with wool wash. Lay flat to block, without stretching. If the texture appears too flat after blocking, place in a dryer set on air fluff for up to 10 minutes to restore the three-dimensional look of the welts.

Weave in loose ends.

Sea Spray Shawl

DESIGNED BY ANGELA TONG

For a shawl that would be easy for beginning knitters without sacrificing on style, **Angela Tong** combined an easy-to-memorize four-row lace pattern—that resembles sprays of water—with systematic yarnover increases in a triangular shape. Worked from the bottom point up to the shoulders with the lacy border included along the way, the length can be customized by simply working more or fewer pattern repeats. Add a few garter rows at the top to prevent curling, bind off, and all that's left is weaving in the ends and blocking open the pretty lace pattern.

FINISHED SIZE

About 52" (132 cm) wide across top edge, and 21½" (54.5 cm) long from top edge to bottom point, blocked.

YARN

Fingering weight (#1 Super Fine).

Shown here: Blue Moon Fiber Arts Socks that Rock Lightweight (100% superwash merino; 405 yd [370 m]/127 g): tanzanite (purple), 2 skeins.

NEEDLES

Size U.S. 6 (4 mm): 40" (100 cm) circular (cir).

Adjust needle size if necessary to obtain the correct gauge.

NOTIONS

Smooth waste yarn for provisional cast-on; markers (m); tapestry needle; blocking pins.

GAUGE

15 sts and 37 rows = 4" (10 cm) in 4-row stitch patt from shawl body, after blocking.

design techniques

Allover lace pattern, page 149.

Triangle worked from bottom to top and shaped with increases, page 146.

Provisional cast-on, page 164.

Yarnover increases, page 168.

Lace edging on sides worked simultaneously with body, page 154.

Garter-stitch edging at top, page 154.

stitch guide

Sl 1 pwise, k2tog, psso: Sl 1 st as if to purl (pwise), k2tog, pass slipped st over—2 sts dec'd. **Note:** Slipping the first stitch pwise deliberately twists it for a decorative effect when the stitch is passed over.

notes

○ Each time you complete Rows 8–11 of the body section, the number of center stitches between the markers will increase by 4. For example, the first time you work Row 8 there are 9 center stitches between the markers (a multiple of 4 sts plus 1). After completing Row 9 the center section increases to 15 stitches (a multiple of 6 sts plus 3) and this count remains unchanged in Row 10. In Row 11, the center section decreases to 13 stitches—4 stitches more than the 9 center stitches in Row 8. The center 13 stitches after completing Row 11 are a multiple of 4 sts plus 5, which is equivalent to a multiple of 4 sts plus 1, so the pattern can repeat again beginning with Row 8.

○ To adjust the finished dimensions, work more or fewer repeats of the 4-row body pattern before working the neck border. Every repeat added or removed will lengthen or shorten the distance between the top edge and bottom point by about ½" (1.3 cm), and will widen or narrow the top edge by about 1" (2.5 cm). You may need more yarn if making a larger shawl.

Shawl

Bottom Point

With smooth waste yarn and using a provisional method (see Glossary), CO 6 sts. Change to main yarn. Work bottom point using short-rows as foll (do not wrap any sts at the turning points):

Set-up row: (WS) Knit.

Row 1: (RS) K1, [yo, k2tog] 2 times, turn work, leaving last st unworked.

Row 2: K5.

Rows 3 and 4: Knit to end.

Rows 5 and 6: Rep Rows 1 and 2.

Row 7: Knit to end, do not turn.

Rotate piece 90 degrees so needle with live sts is to the right and shorter selvedge is at the top. With RS still facing, pick up and knit 1 st from garter ridge in center of selvedge. Rotate work 90 degrees again so provisional CO is at the top. Carefully remove waste yarn from provisional CO, place exposed sts on needle, and work them as k6—13 sts total.

Pattern Set-Up

Set-up row: (WS) K1, yo, k2tog, k3, place marker (pm), p1, pm, k3, k2tog, yo, k1—1 center st; 6 border sts each side.

Row 1: (RS) K2tog, k1, [yo] 2 times, k3, slip marker (sl m), yo, k1, yo, sl m, k3, [yo] 2 times, k1, k2tog—17 sts total; 3 center sts; 7 border sts each side.

Row 2: K2tog, yo, work [k1, p1] in double yo of previous row, k2tog, k1, sl m, p3, sl m, k1, k2tog, work [p1, k1] in double yo of previous row, yo, k2tog—15 sts total; 3 center sts; 6 border sts each side.

Row 3: K6, sl m, yo, k3, yo, sl m, k6—17 sts total; 5 center sts; 6 border sts each side.

Row 4: K1, yo, k2tog, k3, sl m, p5, sl m, k3, k2tog, yo, k1.

Row 5: K2tog, k1, [yo] 2 times, k3, sl m, yo, k1, yo, k3, yo, k1, yo, sl m, k3, [yo] 2 times, k1, k2tog—23 sts total; 9 center sts; 7 border sts each side.

Row 6: K2tog, yo, work [k1, p1] in double yo of previous row, k2tog, k1, sl m, p9, sl m, k1, k2tog, work [p1, k1] in double yo of previous row, yo, k2tog—21 sts total; 9 center sts; 6 border sts each side.

Row 7: K6, sl m, yo, k3, [sl 1 pwise, k2tog, psso (see Stitch Guide)], k3, yo, sl m, k6—still 21 sts.

Body

Row 8: (WS) K1, yo, k2tog, k3, sl m, purl to next m, sl m, k3, k2tog, yo, k1—center sts are a multiple of 4 sts plus 1; 6 border sts each side.

Row 9: (RS) K2tog, k1, [yo] 2 times, k3, sl m, yo, k1, *yo, k3, yo, k1; rep from * to m, yo, sl m, k3, [yo] 2 times, k1, k2tog—center sts have inc'd to a multiple of 6 sts plus 3; 7 border sts each side.

Row 10: K2tog, yo, work [k1, p1] in double yo of previous row, k2tog, k1, sl m, purl to next m, sl m, k1, k2tog, work [p1, k1] in double yo of previous row, yo, k2tog—no change to center sts; 6 border sts each side.

Row 11: K6, sl m, yo, *k3, sl 1 pwise, k2tog, psso; rep from * to 3 sts before next m, k3, yo, sl m, k6—center sts have dec'd to a multiple of 4 sts plus 5; 6 border sts each side; total stitch count is 4 sts more than in Row 8 (see Notes).

Rep Rows 8–11 for patt 43 more times or as desired (see Notes), ending with RS Row 11—197 sts total; 185 center sts; 6 border sts each side.

Neck Border

Knit 5 rows, beg and ending with a WS row.

BO all sts kwise.

Finishing

Weave in loose ends.

Soak in warm water for 20 minutes. Squeeze out water and roll in towels to remove excess moisture. Place on clean, flat surface, and use T-pins to block to measurements. Allow to air-dry thoroughly before removing pins.

Brioche Branches

DESIGNED BY NANCY MARCHANT

Designing new stitch patterns in two-color brioche has become a passion for **Nancy Marchant.** The pretty little branches pattern in this scarf emerges from a combination of increases worked in light-side light-color rows and complementary decreases worked in corresponding dark-side dark-color rows. The result is a different pattern on the two sides of the rectangular scarf—one side is primarily light, the other is primarily dark. Nancy chose to work the scarf in two subtle colors that are close in value to give this design unisex appeal.

FINISHED SIZE

About 7" (18 cm) wide and 72" (183 cm) long.

YARN

Worsted weight (#4 Medium), or two strands of Fingering weight (#1 Super Fine) held together.

Shown here: Brooklyn Tweed Shelter (100% American wool; 140 yd [128 m]/50 g): #25 sap (lime green; LC) and #02 tent (dark green; DC), 2 skeins each.

NEEDLES

Size U.S. 7 (4.5 mm): 16" (40 cm) circular (cir) or set of 2 double-pointed (dpn).

NOTIONS

Markers (m); tapestry needle.

GAUGE

13 sts and 19 rows (counted straight up along a single LSLC knit column) = 4" (10 cm) in two-color brioche patt, using a single strand of the worsted-weight yarn shown.

Note: Exact gauge is not vital for the outcome of this scarf but will affect the density of the fabric.

design techniques

Two-color brioche and patterned brioche stitch, pages 52 and 150.

Flat rectangle worked from tail to tail, page 144.

Two-color Italian cast-on, page 50.

Italian bind-off, page 51.

stitch guide

DS: Dark side of work; dark color forms the knit columns.

LS: Light side of work; light color forms the knit columns.

DC: Dark color; use dark-colored yarn.

LC: Light color; use light-colored yarn.

brk1 (brioche knit or "bark"): K1 (the slipped st of the previous row) tog with its accompanying yo.

brp1 (brioche purl or "burp"): P1 (the slipped st of the previous row) tog with its accompanying yo.

sl1yo: Holding the working yarn in front, sl 1. The way the yarnover is formed depends on whether the slipped stitch follows a knit or brioche-knit stitch, or a purl or brioche-purl stitch.

sl1yo following k or brk: Bring working yarn under the right needle to the front of the work, slip the next stitch purlwise, then bring the yarn over the needle (and over the slipped stitch) to the back of the needle and into position to work the following stitch.

sl1yo following p or brp: With working yarn already in front of the work, slip the next stitch purlwise, then bring the yarn over the needle (and over the slipped stitch) to the front under the needle and into position to work the following stitch.

brkyobrk (brk1, yarnover, brk1): Brk1 but leave the st on the left needle tip, yo by bringing yarn forward under the needle then over the needle to the back, then work brk1 again into the same st—2 sts inc'd.

Note: This turns 1 st into 3 sts, and the 3 sts will be worked as 3 separate stitches on the following row because they have not been "shawled" (see About Brioche Knitting on page 52).

brRsl dec (brioche right-slant decrease): *Sl 1 kwise*, k1, psso, return st just worked to left needle, lift *the st after it* over the returned st and off the needle, then sl the returned st to right needle again—2 sts dec'd; dec slants to right.

Note: The italics indicate an entire shawled stitch; do not separate the stitch from its yarnover.

brLsl dec (brioche left-slant decrease): Sl 1 kwise, brk *next 2 sts tog*, psso—2 sts dec'd; dec slants to left.

Note: The italics indicate 3 loops worked together because one of the 2 stitches is a shawled stitch; do not separate the stitch from its yarnover.

Two-Color Brioche Stitch (odd number of sts)

Note: See above for special abbreviations.

Set-up Row 1 DS LC: With LC, *p1, sl1yo; rep from * to last st, p1, slide sts to other end of needle without turning work.

Set-up Row 2 DS DC: With DC, sl 1, *brk1, sl1yo; rep from * to last 2 sts, brk1, drop DC to back, sl 1, turn work.

Row 1 LS LC: With LC, k1, sl1yo, *brk1, sl1yo; rep from * to last st, k1, slide sts to other end of needle without turning work.

Row 1 LS DC: With DC (hanging in front), sl 1, *brp1, sl1yo; rep from * to last 2 sts, brp1, drop DC to front, sl 1, turn work.

Row 2 DS LC: With LC, p1, sl1yo, *brp1, sl1yo; rep from * to last st, p1, slide sts to other end of needle without turning work.

Row 2 DS DC: With DC (hanging in back), sl 1, *brk1, sl1yo; rep from * to last 2 sts, brk1, drop DC to back, sl 1, turn work.

Rep the Rows 1 and 2 LS and DS for patt (do not rep set-up rows).

Two-Color Branch Stitch
(mult of 4 sts + 3, inc'd to mult of 6 sts + 3)

Note: See page 48 for special abbreviations.

Row 1 LS LC: With LC, k1, sl1yo, *brkyobrk, sl1yo, brk1, sl1yo; rep from * to last st, k1, slide sts to other end of needle without turning work—patt has inc'd to a multiple of 6 sts plus 3.

Row 1 LS DC: With DC (hanging in front), sl 1, brp1, *sl1yo, p1, [sl1yo, brp1] 2 times; rep from * to last st, drop DC to front, sl 1, turn work.

Row 2 DS LC: With LC, p1, sl1yo, *brp1, sl1yo; rep from * to last st, p1, slide sts to other end of needle without turning work.

Row 2 DS DC: With DC (hanging in back), sl 1, *brk1, sl1yo; rep from * to last 2 sts, brk1, drop DC to back, sl 1, turn work.

Row 3 LS LC: With LC, k1, sl1yo, *brk1, sl1yo; rep from * to last st, k1, slide sts to other end of needle without turning work.

Row 3 LS DC: With DC (hanging in front), sl 1, *brp1, sl1yo; rep from * to last 2 sts, brp1, drop DC to front, sl 1, turn work.

Row 4 DS LC: With LC, p1, sl1yo, *brp1, sl1yo; rep from * to last st, p1, slide sts to other end of needle without turning work.

Row 4 DS DC: With DC (hanging in back), sl 1, *brRsl dec, sl1yo, brk1, sl1yo; rep from * to last 2 sts, brk1, drop DC to back, sl 1, turn work—patt has dec'd to a multiple of 4 sts plus 3.

Row 5 LS LC: With LC, k1, sl1yo, *brk1, sl1yo, brkyobrk, sl1yo; rep from * to last st, k1, slide sts to other end of needle without turning work—patt has inc'd to a multiple of 6 sts plus 3.

Row 5 LS DC: With DC (hanging in front), sl 1, brp1, *sl1yo, brp1, sl1yo, p1, sl1yo, brp1; rep from * to last st, drop DC to front, sl 1, turn work.

Row 6 DS LC and DS DC: Rep Rows 2 DS LC and DS DC.

Row 7 LS LC and LS DC: Rep Rows 3 LS LC and LS DC.

Row 8 DS LC: With LC, p1, sl1yo, *brp1, sl1yo; rep from * to last st, p1, slide sts to other end of needle without turning work.

Row 8 DS DC: With DC (hanging in back), sl 1, brk1, *sl1yo, brk1, sl1yo, brLsl dec; rep from * to last st, drop DC to back, sl 1, turn work—patt has dec'd to a multiple of 4 sts plus 3.

Rep Rows 1–8 LS and DS for patt.

notes

○ To familiarize yourself with two-color brioche knitting see pages 66–97 of *Knitting Brioche,* or visit briochestitch.com and, from the Adding Color menu, select Brioche Stitch in Color. You will need to thoroughly understand the specific brioche stitch abbreviations in this pattern. Practice with waste yarn before embarking on a full-size project.

○ Place a removable marker at the beginning of each Row 1 LS LC to help keep track of the pattern.

Scarf

Using the two-color Italian method (see at right), CO 23 sts.

Note: *You can substitute the long-tail method (see Glossary) if you CO with DC over two needles held tog, then remove the extra needle and join LC.*

Work two-color brioche st (see Stitch Guide) until there are 6 LC sts in each knit column on LS of work (the 7th st in the column will be on the needle), ending with Row 2 DS DC.

Work two-color branch st (see Stitch Guide) until piece measures about 71" (180.5 cm) from CO, or 1" (2.5 cm) less than desired finished length, ending with Row 8 DS DC of patt.

Beg with Row 1 LS LC, work two-color brioche st until there are 6 LC sts in each knit column on LS of work (the 7th st in the column will be on the needle) after the end of the branch st patt, ending with Row 2 DS DC.

Using the Italian method (see page 51), BO all sts.

Finishing

Weave in loose ends. Block lightly if desired.

Casting On and Binding Off

Two-color brioche looks best if it is set up during the cast-on and finished with a special bind-off. Follow the instructions here for flexible edges that won't distract from the brioche pattern.

TWO-COLOR ITALIAN CAST-ON

Holding two colors together, make a loose slipknot and place on needle. Holding the slipknot tails out of the way, place the dark color (DC) over your left index finger and the light color (LC) over your thumb, as for the long-tail cast-on (**Figure 1**).

Step 1. To cast on a DC knit stitch, bring the needle tip over the top of LC , under LC, over the top of DC, then under LC and to the front (**Figure 2**).

Step 2. To cast on a LC purl stitch, bring the needle over both strands, then under both, over the top of LC, and back under DC (**Figure 3**).

Repeat Steps 1 and 2 (**Figure 4**) for the desired number of stitches, ending with a knit stitch and not counting the slipknot. Drop the slipknot on the first row of knitting.

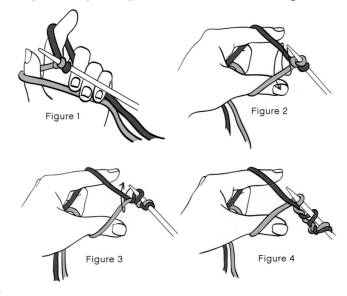

Figure 1

Figure 2

Figure 3

Figure 4

ITALIAN BIND-OFF

Beginning when ready to start a LS LC row, cut both DC and LC, leaving a LC tail four times the width of the knitting to be bound off. Weave in the DC tail as invisibly as possible. With LC threaded on a tapestry needle, work as follows, always keeping the working yarn below the knitting needle and always working the DC yarnover together with its accompanying LC knit stitch:

Step 1. Working from right to left, insert the tapestry purlwise (from right to left) through the first LC knit stitch **(Figure 1)** and pull the yarn snug.

Step 2. Bring the tapestry needle to the back of the work, skip the LC knit stitch, bring the needle to the front between the first two stitches, and then knitwise (from left to right) through the first DC purl stitch **(Figure 2)** and pull the yarn snug.

Step 3. Bring the tapestry needle knitwise through the first LC knit stitch **(Figure 3)** and drop it off the needle.

Step 4. Skip the DC purl stitch, then bring the tapestry needle purlwise through the next LC knit stitch (together with its yarnover; **Figure 4**) and pull the yarn snug.

Step 5. Bring the tapestry needle to the back of the work and insert it from right to left through the back of the first DC purl stitch **(Figure 5)**, pull the yarn snug, and drop this stitch off the needle.

Step 6. With the tapestry needle still in back of the work, skip the first LC knit stitch (and its yarnover), bring the needle to the front between the first two stitches, then knitwise through the DC purl stitch **(Figure 6)**, and pull the yarn snug.

Step 7. Bring the tapestry needle knitwise through the first LC knit stitch (together with its yarnover) and drop it off the needle **(Figure 7)**.

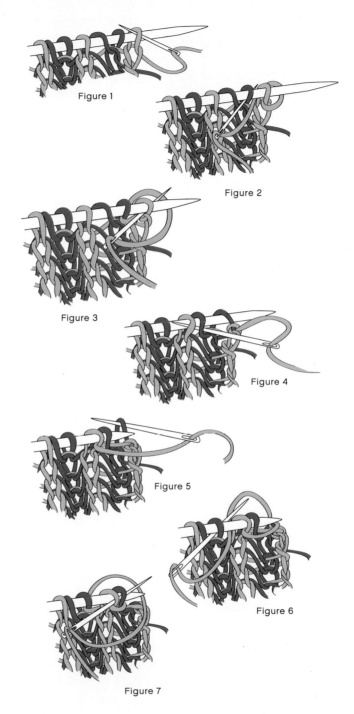

Figure 1

Figure 2

Figure 3

Figure 4

Figure 5

Figure 6

Figure 7

About Brioche Knitting

Brioche knitting creates a cushy, reversible ribbed fabric that is formed by alternating knit and slipped stitches. Instead of carrying the working yarn in front or in back of the slipped stitch, it is carried over the top of the right needle, which adds a "shawl" over the shoulders of the slipped stitch. In the following row, this shawled stitch will be either knitted (called "barked," as in "brk") or purled (called "burped,' as in "brp").

In brioche knitting, a stitch with its yarnover is considered one stitch; do not count the yarnover separately. For example, 4 stitches on the needle will consist of 6 loops of yarn—4 stitches and 2 yarnovers arranged as 2 stitch/yarnover pairs and 2 stitches.

Two-color brioche stitch produces vertical columns of stitches that appear knitted in one color and purled in the other. On the other side of the fabric, the colors are reversed—the knit columns of the first side become the purl columns of the second side, and vice versa. Instead of referring to the right and wrong sides of the work, the reversible faces are referred to as the "light side" (LS) and "dark side" (DS). On the LS, the light color forms the knit columns and the dark color forms the purl stitches; on the DS, the dark color forms the knit columns and the light color forms the purl columns.

Two rows of knitting form one row of the pattern. The first row is denoted "LS LC" (light side; light color) and it is followed by a row worked with the same light side facing but with the dark color and is denoted "LS DC" (light side; dark color). The work is turned so that the dark side (DS) is facing, and two more rows are worked: "DS LC" (dark side; light color) followed by "DS DC" (dark side; dark color). These four rows form the pattern.

To count rows, count the sts in the LS LC columns. Each counted row consists of two rows of actual knitting—one light-side row and one dark-side row.

In brioche color knitting, the yarnovers in the row just worked indicate the color that was used last.

If you use two colors that are close in value, or one color that changes value as you work, designate one to be the LC. Hang a marker on the LC yarn as it comes out of the ball, and place a marker on the LS of the working fabric to help avoid confusion.

If at some point you need to ravel the stitches to fix a mistake, ravel the stitches one at a time and place them onto a smaller circular needle. Remember to change back to the regular-size needle on the next row or round.

Cable-y Cowl

DESIGNED BY PAM ALLEN

A big fan of cables, **Pam Allen** loves the way they lend themselves to tweaking—by varying the background they lay against or by varying the pattern in the crossing stitches. For this cowl, Pam positioned wavy lines of elongated slip stitches against a rustic garter-stitch background to produce a completely reversible fabric. While this cowl is interesting to work from the provisional cast-on to the three-needle bind-off, it isn't tricky and it doesn't demand a lot of attention, which, says Pam, is the best kind of knitting!

FINISHED SIZE

About 7½" (19 cm) wide and 54" (137 cm) in circumference.

YARN

Chunky weight (#5 Bulky).

Shown here: Quince and Company Osprey (100% American wool; 170 yd [155 m]/100 g): #126 lichen, 5 skeins.

NEEDLES

Size U.S. 10½ (6.5 mm): straight.

Adjust needle size if necessary to obtain the correct gauge.

NOTIONS

Waste yarn; cable needle (cn); spare needle same size as main needle; tapestry needle.

GAUGE

44 sts and 50 rows = 7½" (19 cm) in cable-y pattern, after light steaming.

design techniques

Reversible cables, page 148.

Flat rectangle worked from tail to tail and joined into a tube, page 144.

Provisional cast-on, page 164.

Three-needle bind-off, page 162.

stitch guide

<u>5/4LC:</u> Slip 5 sts onto cn and hold in front of work, k4, then from cn work [sl 1, p1] 2 times, sl 1.

<u>4/5RC:</u> Slip 5 sts onto cn and hold in back of work, k4, then from cn work [sl 1, p1] 2 times, sl 1.

<u>4/5LC:</u> Slip 4 sts onto cn and hold in front of work, [sl 1, p1] 2 times, sl 1, then k4 from cn.

<u>5/4RC:</u> Slip 4 sts onto cn and hold in back of work, [sl 1, p1] 2 times, sl 1, then k4 from cn.

Cable-y Pattern (panel of 20 sts)

   Rows 1, 3, and 5: (RS) [Sl 1, p1] 2 times, sl 1, k4, p2, [sl 1, p1] 2 times, sl 1, k4.

   Rows 2, 4, and 6: (WS) K4, [p1, k1] 2 times, p1, k6, [p1, k1] 2 times, p1.

   Row 7: (cable row) [Sl 1, p1] 2 times, sl 1, k4, p2, 5/4LC (see above).

   Rows 8, 10, 12, and 14: [P1, k1] 2 times, p1, k10, [p1, k1] 2 times, p1.

   Rows 9, 11, and 13: [Sl 1, p1] 2 times, sl 1, k4, p2, k4, [sl 1, p1] 2 times, sl 1.

   Row 15: (cable row) 4/5RC (see above), p2, k4, [sl 1, p1] 2 times, sl 1.

   Rows 16, 18, 20, and 22: [P1, k1] 2 times, p1, k6, [p1, k1] 2 times, p1, k4.

   Rows 17, 19, and 21: K4, [sl 1, p1] 2 times, sl 1, p2, k4, [sl 1, p1] 2 times, sl 1.

   Row 23: (cable row) K4, [sl 1, p1] 2 times sl 1, p2, 4/5LC (see at left).

   Rows 24, 26, 28, and 30: K4, [p1, k1] 2 times, p1, k2, [p1, k1] 2 times, p1, k4.

   Rows 25, 27, and 29: K4, [sl 1, p1] 2 times, sl 1, p2, [sl 1, p1] 2 times, sl 1, k4.

   Row 31: (cable row) 5/4RC (see at left), p2, [sl 1, p1] 2 times, sl 1, k4.

   Row 32: Rep Row 2.

   Rep Rows 1–32 for patt.

notes

○ Slipped cable stitches are slipped as if to purl with yarn in back (pwise wyb).

○ In the chart, the slipped cable stitches are shaded blue for the left-crossing cables and pink for the right-crossing cables.

Cowl

With waste yarn and using a provisional method (see Glossary), CO 44 sts. Change to main yarn.

Row 1: (RS) K1 (selvedge st; knit every row), work Row 1 of cable-y patt from chart or Stitch Guide over 20 sts, p2 (center sts; work in rev St st), work Row 1 of cable-y patt over 20 sts, k1 (selvedge st; knit every row).

Row 2: (WS) K1 (selvedge st), work Row 2 of cable-y patt over 20 sts, k2 (center rev St sts), work Row 2 of cable-y patt over 20 sts, k1 (selvedge st).

Knitting the edge sts every row and keeping the center 2 sts in rev St st, cont as established until Rows 1–32 of cable-y patt have been worked 11 times—352 rows completed; piece measures about 54" (137 cm) from CO. Do not cut yarn.

Finishing

Carefully remove waste yarn from provisional CO and place live sts on spare needle—44 sts each on 2 needles. Hold needles parallel with RS of fabric facing tog and WS facing out, being careful not to twist the piece, then use the three-needle method (see Glossary) to BO the sts tog.

Weave in loose ends. Lightly steam to set sts, being careful not to flatten the patt.

Cable-y

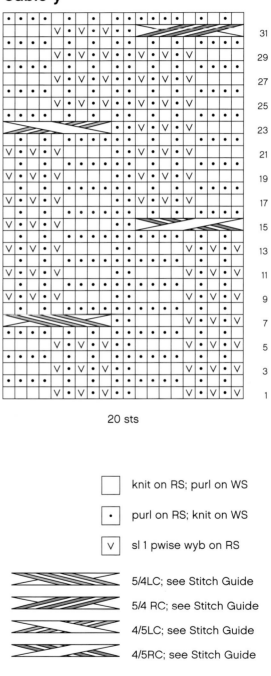

20 sts

☐ knit on RS; purl on WS

• purl on RS; knit on WS

V sl 1 pwise wyb on RS

5/4LC; see Stitch Guide

5/4 RC; see Stitch Guide

4/5LC; see Stitch Guide

4/5RC; see Stitch Guide

Pleated Chevrons

DESIGNED BY VÉRONIK AVERY

Inspired by the Japanese technique of shibori pleating—a process used to create a textural pattern on woven fabrics by binding, stitching, and compression—**Véronik Avery** looked for ways to mimic the look through the use of knit and purl stitches as well as internal increases and decreases. The result is a fairly simple pattern that creates subtle "hinges" that extend from the cast-on at one end to the bind-off at the other and that can be expanded to any width. Worked in pure baby alpaca, this scarf features extraordinary drape and softness.

FINISHED SIZE

9 (13½)" to 10½ (15½)" (23 [34.5] to 26.5 [39.5] cm) wide and 60" (152.5 cm) long.

Stole shown measures 13½" to 15½" (34.5 to 39.5 cm) wide.

YARN

Sportweight (#4 Medium).

Shown here: St-Denis Sommet (100% baby alpaca; 150 yd [137 m]/50 g): #8373 pewter, 4 (6) balls.

NEEDLES

Size U.S. 5 (3.75 mm).

Adjust needle size if necessary to obtain the correct gauge.

NOTIONS

Tapestry needle.

GAUGE

25 sts and 30½ rows = 4" (10 cm) in charted patt.

design techniques

Reversible textured stitch pattern, page 153.

Flat rectangle worked from tail to tail, page 144.

Long-tail cast-on, page 166.

Slipped edge stitches, page 154.

Sewn bind-off, page 162.

stitch guide

<u>K1 below:</u> Insert right needle tip from front to back into the stitch below the next stitch on the left needle, wrap the yarn and knit this loop, then slip the stitch above off the left needle.

<u>P1 below:</u> Insert right needle tip from back to front into the stitch below the next stitch on the left needle, wrap the yarn and purl this loop, then slip the stitch above off the left needle.

notes

○ The numbers for the smaller scarf are given first, followed by the numbers for the wider stole in parentheses. If only one number or measurement is given, it applies to both the scarf and stole.

○ In order to cast on sufficiently loose stitches, allow about ¼" (6 mm) between each pair of stitches as you cast on. Alternatively, use a provisional method to cast on, and then use the sewn method to bind off the live stitches at each end of the scarf during finishing.

○ For selvedge stitches, slip the first stitch of every row as if to purl with yarn in front (pwise wyf) and knit the last stitch of every row (as shown on the chart).

Scarf or Stole

Using the long-tail method (see Glossary), very loosely (see Notes) CO 65 (97) sts.

Set-up row: (WS) Work the set-up row of Herringbone chart, working the 16-st patt rep 3 (5) times.

Rows 1–20: Work Rows 1–4 of chart 5 times.

Rows 21–24: Work Rows 5–8 of chart once, dec in Row 8 as shown—57 (85) sts rem.

Rows 25–44: Work Rows 9–12 of chart 5 times.

Rows 45–48: Work Rows 13–16 of chart once, inc in Row 16 as shown—65 (97) sts.

Rows 49–68: Work Rows 17–20 of chart 5 times.

Rep Rows 21–68 eight more times (do not rep Rows 1–20), then work Rows 17–19 of chart once more, ending with a RS row—456 rows total, including set-up row. Cut yarn, leaving a 42 (62)" (106.5 [157.5] cm) tail.

Herringbone

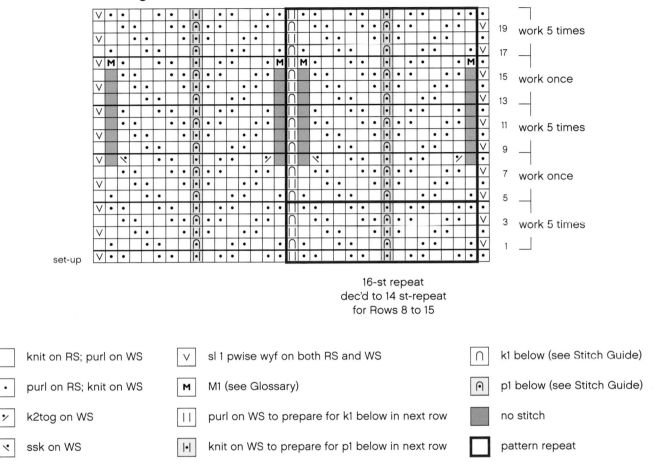

16-st repeat
dec'd to 14 st-repeat
for Rows 8 to 15

set-up

19 work 5 times
17
15 work once
13
11 work 5 times
9
7 work once
5
3 work 5 times
1

	knit on RS; purl on WS	V	sl 1 pwise wyf on both RS and WS	∩	k1 below (see Stitch Guide)
•	purl on RS; knit on WS	M	M1 (see Glossary)	⋒	p1 below (see Stitch Guide)
⟍	k2tog on WS	‖	purl on WS to prepare for k1 below in next row	▨	no stitch
⟍	ssk on WS	•│	knit on WS to prepare for p1 below in next row	☐	pattern repeat

Finishing

Thread tail on a tapestry needle and use the sewn method (see Glossary) to BO all sts loosely.

Weave in loose ends. Block to measurements.

Cross Timbers

DESIGNED BY ALEXIS WINSLOW

Inspired by the Northern Cross Timbers, an area in central Oklahoma that separates rolling prairie lands to the west from vast oak forests to the east, **Alexis Winslow** chose a horizontal zigzag motif with intertwining diamonds for this two-color cowl. Worked in stranded colorwork that creates yarn floats along the wrong side, the fabric provides double protection against the cold and wind. Edged with a bit of ribbing and a reverse stockinette roll, the bold pattern will hold your interest from cast-on to bind-off.

FINISHED SIZE

About 17 (19½, 22)" (43 [49.5, 56] cm) in circumference and 11" (28 cm) tall.

Cowl shown measures 19½" (49.5 cm).

YARN

Worsted weight (#4 Medium).

Shown here: Berroco Ultra Alpaca (50% alpaca, 50% wool; 215 yd [197 m]/100 g): #62171 berry pie mix (A) and #62168 candy floss mix (B), 1 skein each.

NEEDLES

Size U.S. 6 (4 mm): set of 4 or 5 double-pointed (dpn).

Adjust needle size if necessary to obtain the correct gauge.

NOTIONS

Markers (m); tapestry needle.

GAUGE

19¾ sts and 28 rnds = 4" (10 cm) in charted pattern, worked in rnds and slightly relaxed after blocking.

design techniques

Fair Isle pattern, page 151.

Short tube worked from the bottom up, page 145.

Long-tail cast-on, page 166.

Ribbed edges with small reverse stockinette-stitch roll, page 154.

Elastic bind-off, page 155.

notes

○ When working the corrugated two-color rib, carry the unused color very loosely on the wrong side of the work to avoid puckering.

○ To make working the charted pattern easier, place a marker after every pattern repeat, if desired.

Cowl

With A and using the long-tail method (see Glossary), CO 84 (96, 108) sts. Place marker (pm) and join for working in rnds, being careful not to twist sts.

Purl 2 rnds.

Join B and work corrugated rib as foll:

Set-up rnd: K1 with A, *k2 with B, k2 with A; rep from * to last 3 sts, k2 with B, k1 with A.

Rib rnd: K1 with A, *p2 with B, k2 with A; rep from * to last 3 sts, p2 with B, k1 with A.

Rep the rib rnd 5 more times—piece measures about 1½" (3.8 cm) from CO.

Work Rnds 1–55 of Cross Timbers chart, working the 12-st patt rep 7 (8, 9) times around—piece measures about 9½" (24 cm) from CO.

Work set-up rnd, then 6 rnds of corrugated rib patt as before.

Cut B. Cont with A only, knit 1 rnd, then purl 2 rnds—piece measures 11" (28 cm) from CO.

Loosely BO all sts pwise (use a larger needle, if necessary, to ensure elasticity of BO edge).

Finishing

Weave in loose ends. Block to measurements.

Cross Timbers

	knit with A
⊠	knit with B
□	pattern repeat

12-st repeat

Star Palatine

DESIGNED BY GALINA KHMELEVA

For a confluence of the traditional and modern in this lacy shawl, **Galina Khmeleva** used a traditional Orenburg diagonal element to form the star motifs in the center, but she tapered the cast-on and bind-off edges into points to instill a more modern look to the classic rectangular palatine shape. She also substituted kid mohair in a rich burgundy for the more traditional natural white. Knitted against a garter-stitch foundation—no purling!—this shawl features a sawtooth edging that is worked simultaneously with the body. A simple slipped stitch borders each edge.

FINISHED SIZE

About 20" (51 cm) wide and 75½" (192 cm) long, blocked.

YARN

Fingering weight (#1 Super Fine).

Shown here: Filatura Di Crosa Baby Kid Extra (80% baby kid mohair, 20% polyamid; 268 yd [245 m]/25 g): #500 mulberry, 4 balls.

NEEDLES

Size U.S. 5 (3.75 mm).

Adjust needle size if necessary to obtain the correct gauge.

NOTIONS

Contrasting waste yarn for provisional cast-on; markers (m) in two different colors; tapestry needle; smooth, thin nylon cord; blocking wires and T-pins.

GAUGE

About 20 sts and 30½ rows = 4" (10 cm) in average gauge from charted patts, after blocking.

☐ knit on both RS and WS		⌒ BO 1 st	
○ yo		☐ st rem on right needle after BO	
╱ k2tog		+ k1 and return st to left needle	
⋏ k3tog		− unworked st	
⩛ sl 1 pwise wyf on both RS and WS		‖ marker positions	

Shawl

With contrasting waste yarn and working yarn held tog, cast on provisionally as foll: Make a slipknot and place on two needles held tog. With waste yarn around your thumb and working yarn around your index finger, use the long-tail method (see Glossary) to CO 7 sts (the slip-knot does not count as a st).

Carefully remove one needle from the CO and cont working with one needle at a time in the usual manner.

Lower Corner

Set-up row: (WS) Sl 1 pwise wyf, k6, drop slipknot from needle, turn work.

Row 1: (RS) Sl 1 pwise wyf, k2, yo, k1, yo, k2tog and return this st to left needle, leaving last corner st unworked—2 sts on left needle; 8 sts total.

Rows 2, 4, 6, 8, and 10: Knit to end.

Row 3: Sl 1 pwise wyf, [k2, yo] 2 times, k2tog and return this st to left needle, leaving last st unworked—2 sts on left needle; 9 sts total.

Row 5: Sl 1 pwise wyf, k2, yo, k3, yo, k2tog and return this st to left needle, leaving last st unworked—2 sts on left needle; 10 sts total.

Row 7: Sl 1 pwise wyf, k2, yo, k4, yo, k2tog. You will now be at the gap created by turning before the last st in Rows 1, 3, and 5. To close this gap, insert the left needle tip from front to back into one edge loop in the center of the gap and lift this loop onto the left needle. Work the lifted loop tog with the last corner st as k2tog, then return this st to left needle—1 st on left needle; 11 sts total.

Row 9: Sl 1 pwise wyf, k2, yo, k5, yo, k2tog and return this st to left needle, leaving last st unworked—2 sts on left needle; 12 sts total.

Row 11: BO 5 sts (1 st rem on right needle after last BO), k2, yo, k1, yo, k2tog and return this st to left needle, leaving last st unworked—2 sts on left needle; 8 sts total.

Row 12: Knit to end—8 sts; lower corner is complete.

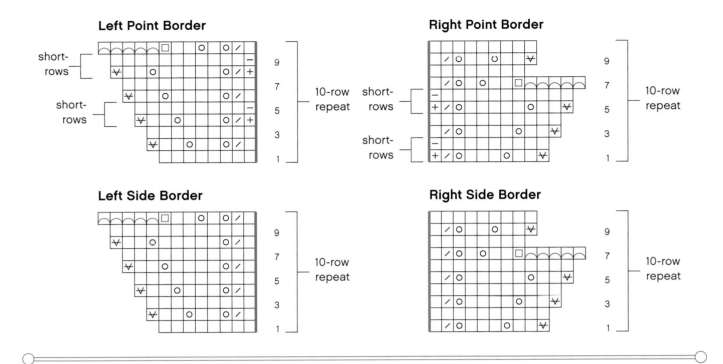

Left Point Border

short-rows

short-rows

10-row repeat

Right Point Border

short-rows

short-rows

10-row repeat

Left Side Border

10-row repeat

Right Side Border

10-row repeat

Lower Point

Set-up Row 1: (RS) Sl 1 pwise wyf, [k2, yo] 2 times, k2tog, k1, place marker (pm). Temporarily turn work so WS is facing and slip an empty needle into the 3 loops along the selvedge of the lower point corner. Turn work so RS is facing again and work the 3 lifted loops as k1tbl, k2tog tbl, pm—11 sts total; 9 sts before first m, 2 sts between m. Temporarily turn work so WS is facing and slip an empty needle into the 7 loops from the base of the CO. Leave waste yarn in place to identify the left side of the border (it can be removed during finishing). Turn work so RS is facing again and knit across the 7 CO sts—18 sts total; 9 sts before first m; 2 sts between m; 7 sts after second m.

Set-up Row 2: (WS) Sl 1 pwise wyf, k2, yo, k1, yo, k2tog, k1, slip marker (sl m), k2, sl m, k9—19 sts total; with RS facing there will be 9 sts before first m, 2 sts between m, and 8 sts after second m.

Note: *For the right border (at beginning of RS rows), the pattern rows are odd-numbered RS rows, and the "return" rows are even-numbered WS rows. For the left border (at beginning of WS rows), the pattern rows are even-numbered WS rows, and the "return" rows are odd-numbered RS rows.*

Note: *The borders along the diagonal sides of the point need to be longer than the borders along the straight vertical sides so that the diagonal edges will lie flat without puckering. To accommodate this, each point border chart contains two pairs of short-rows (4 extra rows total) that are worked on the border stitches only. Because of the extra short-rows, each 10-row repeat of a point border chart corresponds to 6 rows worked across the center section of the shawl.*

Work the next 6 rows of the center section with 10 border rows at each side as foll:

Lower Point

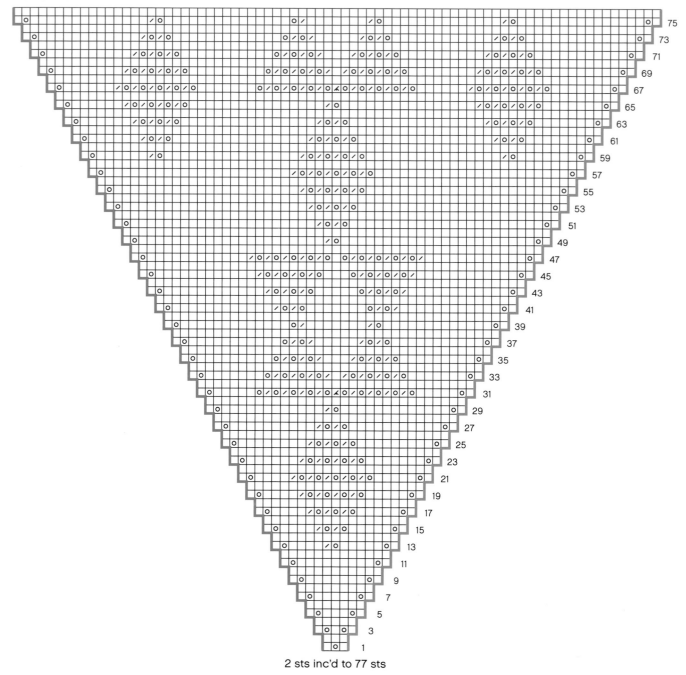

2 sts inc'd to 77 sts

Body, Rows 77 to 112

Row numbers on right side: 111, 109, 107, 105, 103, 101, 99, 97, 95, 93, 91, 89, 87, 85, 83, 81, 79, 77

36-row repeat

work 5 times

77 sts

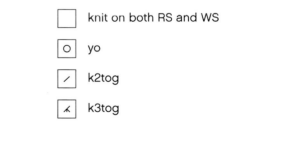

	knit on both RS and WS
o	yo
∕	k2tog
⋏	k3tog

Row 1: (RS; right border short-rows) Work Row 1 of Right Point Border chart, return last st to left needle, turn, knit to end for Row 2 of chart, turn—2 short-rows completed on right border. With RS facing, work Row 3 of Right Point Border chart, sl m, work Row 1 of Lower Point chart over 2 sts while inc them to 3 sts, sl m, work Row 1 of Left Point Border chart—22 sts total; 11 sts right border; 3 center sts; 8 sts left border.

Row 2: (WS) Work Row 2 of Left Point Border chart over 8 sts while inc them to 9 sts, sl m, work Row 2 of Lower Point chart over 3 sts, sl m, work Row 4 of Right Point Border chart—23 sts total; 11 sts right border; 3 center sts; 9 sts left border.

Row 3: (right border short-rows) Work Row 5 of Right Point Border chart, return last st to left needle, turn, knit to end for Row 6 of chart, turn—2 short-rows completed on right border. With RS facing, work Row 7 of Right Point Border chart, sl m, work Row 3 of Lower Point chart over

3 sts while inc them to 5 sts, sl m, work Row 3 of Left Point Border chart—22 sts total; 8 sts right border; 5 center sts; 9 sts left border.

Row 4: (left border short-rows) Work Row 4 of Left Point Border chart, return last st to left needle, turn, knit to end for Row 5 of chart, turn—2 short-rows completed on left border. With WS facing, work Row 6 of Left Point Border chart, sl m, work Row 4 of Lower Point chart over 5 sts, sl m, work Row 8 of Right Point Border chart—24 sts total; 8 sts right border; 5 center sts; 11 sts left border.

Row 5: Work Row 9 of Right Point Border chart, sl m, work Row 5 of Lower Point chart over 5 sts while inc them to 7 sts, sl m, work Row 7 of Left Point Border chart—27 sts total; 9 sts right border; 7 center sts; 11 sts left border.

Row 6: (left border short-rows) Work Row 8 of Left Point Border chart, return last st to left needle, turn, knit to end for Row 9 of chart, turn—2 short-rows completed on left border. With WS facing, work Row 10 of Left Point Border chart, sl m, work Row 6 of Lower Point chart over 7 sts, sl m, work Row 10 of Right Point Border chart—24 sts total; 9 sts right border; 7 center sts; 8 sts left border; 10 rows completed for each border in 6 center rows.

Note: *As you work the following instructions, you may find it helpful to use separate row counters or another method to keep track of the rows in the individual borders and the center section.*

Cont in this manner, working 10 border rows for every 6 rows in the center section, until Row 76 of the Lower Point chart has been completed, ending with Row 8 of right border and Row 6 of left border—96 sts total; 8 sts right border; 77 center sts; 11 sts left border.

Shawl Body

Note: *For the straight-sided body of the shawl, the borders are worked without short-rows; every row is worked across all stitches.*

Transition from working the Right and Left Point Border charts to the Right and Left Side Border charts as foll:

Next row: (RS) Work Row 9 of Right Side Border chart to m, sl m, work Row 77 of Body chart over 77 sts, sl m, work Row 7 of Left Side Border chart to end—97 sts total; 9 sts right border; 77 center sts; 11 sts left border.

Cont side border patts as established, work Rows 78–112 of Body chart once, then work Rows 77–112 four more times, ending with Row 8 of right border and Row 6 of left border—180 rows completed from first section of Body chart; 96 sts total; 8 sts right border; 77 center sts; 11 sts left border.

Cont border patts as established, work Rows 113–146 of Body chart once, ending with Row 2 of right border and Row 10 of left border—34 rows completed from middle section of Body chart; 95 sts total; 10 sts right border; 77 center sts; 8 sts left border.

Cont border patts as established, work Rows 147–182 of Body chart 5 times, ending with Row 2 of right border and Row 10 of left border—180 rows completed from last section of Body chart; 394 Body chart rows total; 95 sts; 10 sts right border; 77 center sts; 8 sts left border.

Top Point

Note: *For the top point, the borders are worked with short-rows as for the lower point.*

Transition from working the Right and Left Side Border charts to the Right and Left Point Border charts as foll:

Next row: (RS) Work Row 3 of Right Point Border chart to m, sl m, work Row 183 of Top Point chart (see page 75) over 77 sts while dec them to 75 sts, sl m, work Row 1 of Left Point Border chart to end—94 sts total; 11 sts right border; 75 center sts; 8 sts left border.

Cont border patts with short-rows as established until Row 258 of the Top Point chart has been completed, ending with Row 8 of right border and Row 6 of left border—76 rows completed from Top Point chart; 21 sts rem; 8 sts right border; 2 center sts; 11 sts left border.

Top Point Corner

Work back and forth in rows on right border sts as foll:

Row 1: (RS) Sl 1 pwise wyf, [k2, yo] 2 times, k2tog and return this st to left needle, leaving last right border st unworked—2 right border sts on left needle; 9 right border sts total.

Rows 2, 4, 6, and 8: Knit to end.

Row 3: Sl 1 pwise wyf, k2, yo, k3, yo, k2tog and return this st to left needle, do not work last st—2 right border sts on left needle; 10 right border sts total.

Row 5: Sl 1 pwise wyf, k2, yo, k4, yo, k2tog. You will now be at the gap created by turning before the last border st in Rows 1 and 3. To close this gap, insert the left needle tip from front to back into one edge loop in the center of the gap and lift this loop onto the left needle. Removing the marker as you come to it, work the lifted loop tog with the last corner st and the first shawl body st after it as k3tog, then return this st to left needle—1 right border st on left needle; 11 right border sts total.

Row 7: Sl 1 pwise wyf, k2, yo, k5, yo, k2tog and return this st to left needle, leaving last right border st unworked—2 right border sts on left needle; 12 right border sts total.

Row 9: BO 5 sts (1 st rem on right needle after last BO), k2, yo, k1, yo, k2tog, work last border st tog with 1 rem shawl body st as k2tog—8 right border sts rem; no shawl body sts; 11 left border sts unworked on left needle. Do not turn.

With RS still facing, cont on left border sts as foll:

Next row: (RS) Work Row 7 of Left Point Border chart over 11 left border sts.

Next row: (left border short-rows) Work Row 8 of Left Point Border chart, return last st to left needle, turn, knit to end for Row 9 of chart, turn, work Row 10 of Left Point Border chart—8 sts rem for each border; 16 sts total.

Cut yarn, leaving a 12" (30.5 cm) tail.

Finishing

With tail threaded on a tapestry needle, use the Kitchener st (see Glossary) to graft the two sets of 8 sts tog.

Weave in loose ends.

Blocking

Beg at one corner and using nylon cord threaded on a tapestry needle, thread nylon cord loosely from back to front through each tooth point, then tie the ends of the cord tog, leaving a generous amount of slack to accommodate the size of the blocked shawl. Thoroughly wet the piece and squeeze out excess moisture. Lay the piece on a clean flat surface. Use T-pins to pin the four corners of the straight-sided section of shawl body to about 20" (51 cm) wide and 51½" (131 cm) long. Pin the tip of each corner point so it is about 12" (30.5 cm) from the first or last row of the straight-sided main section—piece measures about 75½" (192 cm) total from tip to tip. Run a separate length of cord all the way around the six T-pins to form a lozenge-shaped outline that will act as a blocking guide. Pull cord threaded through the shawl between each pair of teeth out to meet the blocking guide cord and anchor with a T-pin. Always pin into the nylon cord loops, not into the project itself. Adjust the pins and cord as necessary until the shawl is stretched taut to the guide cord outline. Allow to air-dry thoroughly before moving the pins and cords.

Body, Rows 113 to 146

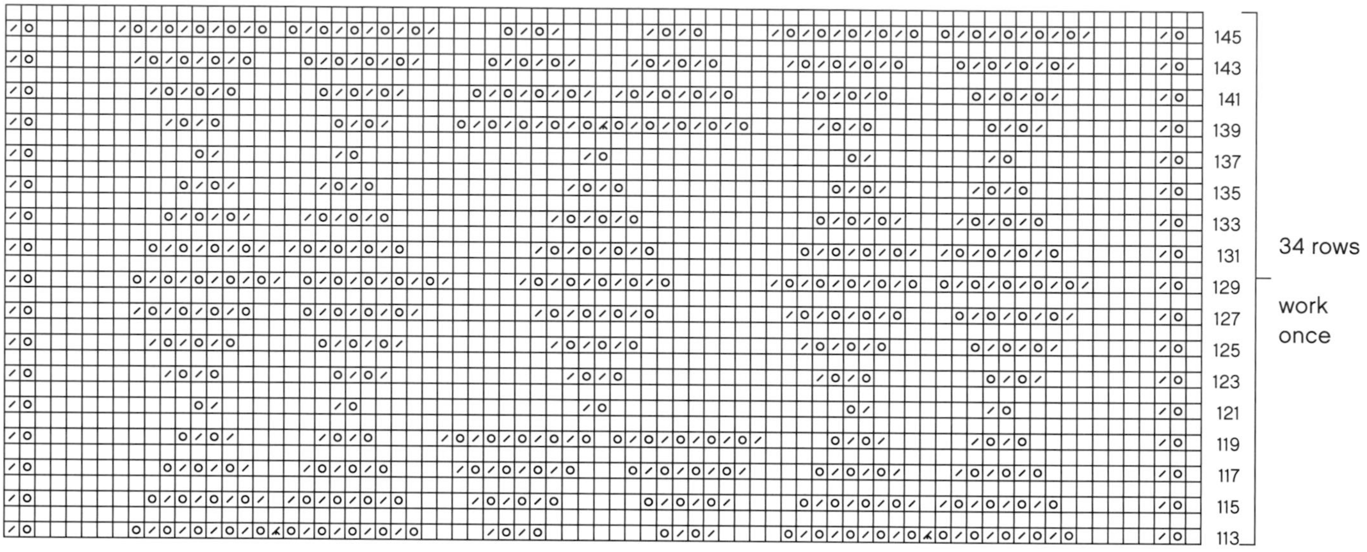

145
143
141
139
137
135
133
131
129
127
125
123
121
119
117
115
113

34 rows

work once

77 sts

Body, Rows 147 to 182

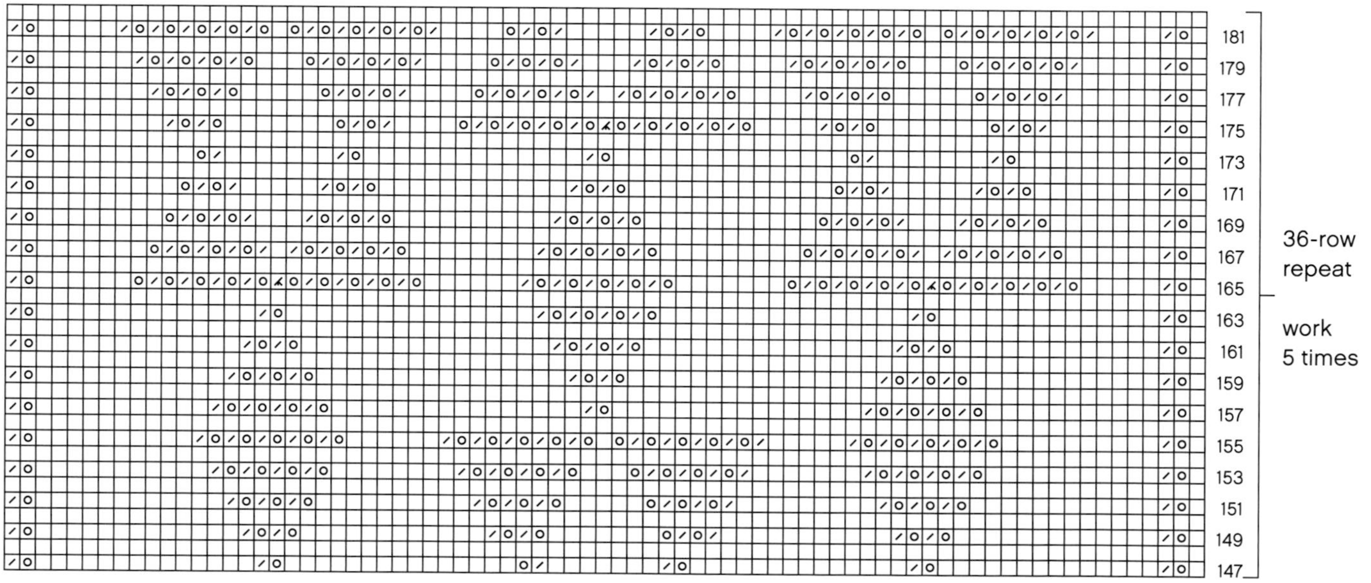

181
179
177
175
173
171
169
167
165
163
161
159
157
155
153
151
149
147

36-row repeat

work 5 times

77 sts

Top Point

knit on both RS and WS

○ yo

╱ k2tog

⋌ k3tog

| | marker positions

257
255
253
251
249
247
245
243
241
239
237
235
233
231
229
227
225
223
221
219
217
215
213
211
209
207
205
203
201
199
197
195
193
191
189
187
185
183

77 sts dec'd to 2 sts

Tubular Fair Isle

DESIGNED BY DEBORAH NEWTON

For this thick and cozy scarf, **Deborah Newton** combined seven colors of worsted-weight alpaca in Fair Isle patterns that she worked in rounds so that the stranded yarns along the wrong side of the fabric would be enclosed within the resulting tube. By adding texture in the form of an occasional purl stitch, she instilled an updated look to the otherwise traditional pattern motifs. To give the piece a bit of whimsy, she added garter-stitch points to the ends and topped them off with mismatched chunky tassels.

FINISHED SIZE

About 7½" (19 cm) wide and 63" (160 cm) long, excluding tassels.

YARN

Worsted weight (#4 Medium).

Shown here: Alpaca with a Twist Highlander (45% baby alpaca, 45% merino, 8% microfiber, 2% viscose; 145 yd [133 m]/100 g): #5014 ochre (dark orange; A), 2 skeins; #5013 fritillary (light orange; B), #0203 sandy beach (tan; C), #2010 wild pansy (light purple; D), #1013 north sea (light blue; E), #4011 lady fern (green; F), and #3016 tartan red (burgundy; G), 1 skein each.

Note: The scarf shown used almost the entire skein of color B.

NEEDLES

Size U.S. 9 (5.5 mm): 16" (40 cm) circular (cir) or set of 4 or 5 double-pointed (dpn) and three straight needles for working ends (if not using dpn; see Notes).

Adjust needle size if necessary to obtain the correct gauge.

NOTIONS

Marker (m); tapestry needle.

GAUGE

19 sts and 21 rnds = 4" (10 cm) in charted patt, worked in rnds.

design techniques

Combined Fair Isle patterns, page 151.

Long tube worked from tail to tail, page 144.

Provisional cast-on, page 164.

Paired decrease shaping, page 158.

Tassels, page 170.

notes

○ This scarf is knitted in the round, then the tube is flattened, and each end is closed with a triangular section of garter stitch.

○ The body of the scarf may be worked on a 16" (40 cm) circular needle or a set of double-pointed needles as you prefer. The ends of the tube are closed using three double-pointed or straight needles and the garter-stitch end triangles are worked back and forth in rows using those same needles.

○ Carry the yarn not in use loosely across the back of the work, twisting the colors around each other as necessary to prevent long floats from forming.

○ When joining a new color, twist the new yarn with the working yarn over a few stitches before beginning to knit with the new color. This automatically weaves in the starting end. Trim the starting tail to 1" to 2" (2.5 to 5 cm) long and leave it hanging on the inside of the scarf tube.

Scarf

With A and cir needle or dpn, use a provisional method (see Glossary) to CO 72 sts. Place marker (pm) and join for working in rnds, being careful not to twist sts.

Work Rnds 1–154 of Fair Isle chart once, then work Rnds 1–89 once more, then knit 1 rnd with A—244 rnds total; piece measures about 46½" (118 cm) from CO.

Do not cut yarn.

Close End of Tube

Flatten tube so beg of rnd is aligned with the fold at one side, then rearrange sts with 36 sts each on two separate dpn or straight needles for the front and back of the scarf. Hold needles tog and parallel, with working strand of A at tip of one needle.

Joining row: With A and a third needle, *insert right needle tip into first st on each of the parallel needles and work them tog as k2tog (1 st from each needle); rep from * to end—36 sts rem on one needle.

Next row: Knit and *at the same time* dec 5 sts evenly spaced—31 sts rem.

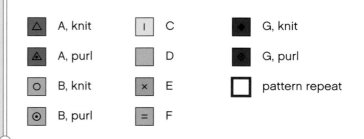

△ A, knit	I C	◆ G, knit
▲ A, purl	D	◇ G, purl
○ B, knit	× E	☐ pattern repeat
⊙ B, purl	= F	

Fair Isle

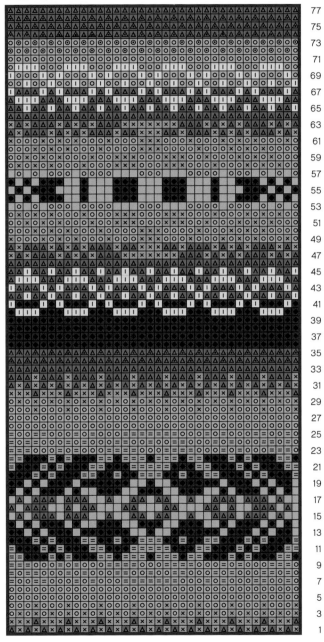

77
75
73
71
69
67
65
63
61
59
57
55
53
51
49
47
45
43
41
39
37
35
33
31
29
27
25
23
21
19
17
15
13
11
9
7
5
3
1

36-st repeat
work 2 times

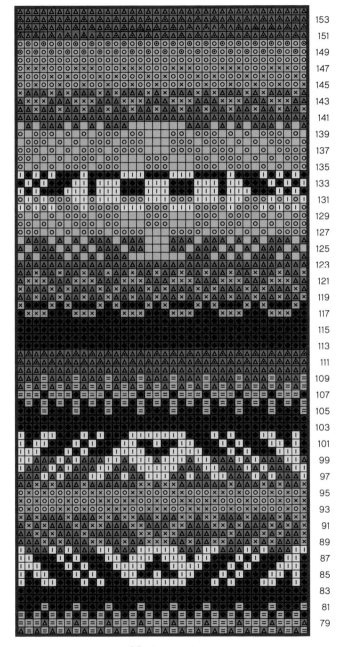

153
151
149
147
145
143
141
139
137
135
133
131
129
127
125
123
121
119
117
115
113
111
109
107
105
103
101
99
97
95
93
91
89
87
85
83
81
79

36-st repeat
work 2 times

End Triangles

Note: *When working the triangle shaping, you may find it helpful to mark one side of the work as the RS with waste yarn or a safety pin.*

Row 1: (RS; dec row) K2, ssk, knit to last 4 sts, k2tog, k2—2 sts dec'd.

Rows 2–4: Knit 3 rows, beg and ending with a WS row.

Rep the last 4 rows 12 more times—5 sts rem.

BO while working rem sts as k1, k3tog, k1 in the BO row— no sts rem; triangle measures about 8¼" (21 cm) from joining row.

Carefully remove waste yarn from CO edge and arrange 72 exposed sts for the second end of the scarf as 36 sts each on two needles. Check to make sure the fold lines at each side of the scarf are aligned with the first end, rearranging sts as necessary. Close the other end of the tube and work an end triangle the same as for the first end of the scarf.

Finishing
Tassels (make 2)

Make two 3" (7.5 cm) tassels (see Glossary), one each in colors E and F. Attach one tassel to the tip of each triangle as shown.

Steam-block lightly if desired, taking care not to touch the iron to the fabric, and allow steam to permeate fabric. Flatten slightly with fingers and palms and allow to air-dry completely before moving.

Sylvie Scarf

DESIGNED BY COURTNEY KELLEY

In an attempt to capture and counteract winter's bleakness, **Courtney Kelley** chose a pattern reminiscent of snowflakes and flowers for one face of this reversible scarf and a simple salt-and-pepper pattern for the other. The scarf is knitted in a tube, but thanks to a column of slipped stitches along each side, it folds flat to keep the two patterns separate. Corrugated ribbing adds contrasting interest to the ends. Knitted in a blend of baby alpaca, merino, and bamboo in soft, cool colors, this scarf features beautiful drape and luxurious warmth.

FINISHED SIZE

About 5½" (14 cm) wide and 68" (172.5 cm) long, blocked.

YARN

Fingering weight (#1 Super Fine).

Shown here: The Fibre Company Canopy Fingering (50% baby alpaca, 30% merino, 20% bamboo; 200 yd [183 m]/50 g): palm bud (light blue-gray; MC), 3 skeins; plum (CC), 2 skeins.

NEEDLES

Corrugated rib: size U.S. 2 (2.75 mm): 16" (40 cm) circular (cir) needle.

Body: size U.S. 3 (3 mm): 16" (40 cm) cir needle.

Adjust needle size if necessary to obtain the correct gauge.

NOTIONS

Size C/2 (3 mm) crochet hook and smooth waste yarn for provisional cast-on; markers (m); spare needle same size as smaller cir needle; tapestry needle.

GAUGE

36½ sts and 29½ rnds = 4" (10 cm) in salt-and-pepper and charted patterns with larger needle, worked in rnds.

design techniques

Combined Fair Isle patterns, page 151.

Long tube worked from tail to tail, page 144.

Provisional cast-on, page 164.

Ribbed edging, page 154.

stitch guide

Salt-and-Pepper Pattern (odd number of sts)

Rnd 1: *K1 with CC, k1 with MC; rep from * to last st, k1 with CC.

Rnd 2: *K1 with MC, k1 with CC; rep from * to last st, k1 with MC.

Rep Rnds 1 and 2 for patt.

note

○ When changing colors in the charted pattern, always bring CC *under* MC into position for working the next stitch, and always bring MC *over* CC into working position.

Scarf

With MC and larger cir needle, use the crochet chain provisional method (see Glossary) to CO 100 sts. Place marker (pm) and join for working in rnds, being careful not to twist sts.

Set-up rnd: K1 with MC, work set-up rnd of Sylvie chart over 49 sts, pm, k1 with MC, work Rnd 1 of salt-and-pepper patt (see Stitch Guide) over 49 sts.

Next rnd: K1 with MC, work next rnd of chart over 49 sts, slip marker (sl m), k1 with MC, work Rnd 2 of salt-and-pepper patt over 49 sts.

Next rnd: Sl 1 purlwise with yarn in back (pwise wyb), work next rnd of chart over 49 sts, sl m, sl 1 pwise wyb, work Rnd 1 of salt-and-pepper patt over 49 sts.

Rep the last 2 rnds until Rnds 1–24 of chart have been worked a total of 20 times (do not rep the set-up rnd)—481 rnds completed; piece measures about 65" (165 cm) from CO.

Ribbed Edgings

Change to smaller cir needle and work corrugated rib as foll:

Rnd 1: *K1 with MC, [p1 with CC, k1 with MC] 24 times, p1 with CC, sl m; rep from, * once more.

Rnd 2: *Sl 1 pwise wyb, [p1 with CC, k1 with MC] 24 times, p1 with CC, sl m; rep from * once more.

Rep the last 2 rnds until rib measures 1½" (3.8 cm) from end of chart. Place first 50 sts onto spare needle and hold the needles parallel with WS facing tog and RS facing out—50 sts each on two needles. With CC and smaller cir needle, use the three-needle method (see Glossary) to BO the two sets of sts tog.

Turn scarf inside out and weave in loose ends. Turn scarf right side out again.

Carefully remove waste yarn from provisional CO, and place 100 exposed sts on smaller cir needle. Rejoin yarns at one side so the first st to be worked is from a slip-st

column. Beg with Rnd 2, work corrugated rib patt as before until rib measures 1½" (3.8 cm) from provisional CO. Place first 50 sts onto spare needle and close the second end of the scarf in the same manner as the first end.

Finishing

Weave in remaining ends from second ribbed edging. Block to measurements.

Sylvie

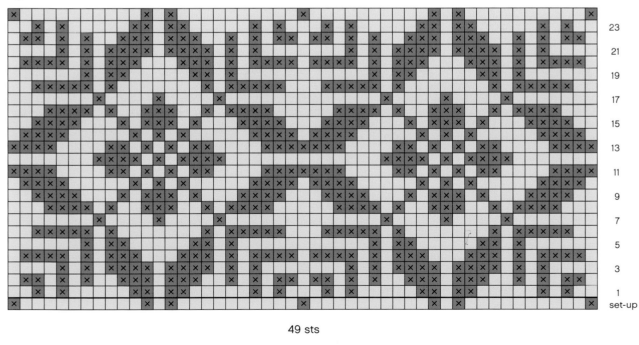

49 sts

☐ knit with MC   ☒ knit with CC   ☐ pattern repeat

Deep Shade Scarf

DESIGNED BY JOLENE TREACE

To plan the pattern proportions in this rectangular shawl, **JoLene Treace** employed the Fibonacci series—a numerical sequence that abounds in nature. Beginning with 0 and 1, each number in the series is the sum of the previous two (0, 1, 1, 2, 3, 5, 8, 13, 21, and so on). The main component of JoLene's scarf is an eight-stitch garter-and-faggoting section containing three garter stitches, two faggoting stitches, and three garter stitches. These eight-stitch panels alternate with twenty-stitch leaf panels. For the side borders JoLene added three more garter stitches plus a chained (slipped) selvedge stitch.

FINISHED SIZE

About 11½" (29 cm) wide and 65" (165 cm) long, relaxed after blocking.

YARN

Fingering weight (#1 Super Fine).

Shown here: Handmaiden Sea Silk (70% silk, 30% seacell; 437 yd [400 m]/100 g): cedar, 2 skeins.

NEEDLES

Size U.S. 4 (3.5 mm).

Adjust needle size if necessary to obtain the correct gauge.

NOTIONS

Tapestry needle.

GAUGE

29 sts and 56 rows (1 patt rep wide and 2 patt reps high) from Deep Shade chart measure 4½" (11.5 cm) wide and 6½" (16.5 cm) high, relaxed after blocking.

design techniques

Combined lace patterns, page 149.

Flat rectangle worked from tail to tail, page 144.

Elastic cast-on, page 155.

Garter borders on all sides, page 154.

Slipped edge stitches, page 154.

notes

○ The first and last stitch of every row is a chained selvedge stitch. Work the selvedge stitches by slipping the first stitch of every row purlwise with the yarn in front (pwise wyf) and knit the last stitch of every row.

○ The second skein of yarn was joined using the Russian method (see page 157), leaving only the starting and ending yarn tails to be woven in during finishing.

Scarf

Using an elastic method (see page 155), loosely CO 74 sts.

Bottom Border

Border row: Sl 1 pwise wyf (see Notes), knit to end.

Rep this row 15 more times—16 border rows total and 8 garter ridges completed.

Center

Work Rows 1–28 of Deep Shade chart 19 times, then work Rows 29–38 once—542 chart rows completed.

Top Border

Border row: Sl 1 pwise wyf, knit to end.

Rep this row 15 more times—16 border rows total and 8 garter ridges completed.

Loosely BO all sts.

Finishing

Weave in loose ends. Block to about 13" (33 cm) wide and 65" (165 cm) long; scarf will relax to about 11½" (29 cm) wide.

Deep Shade

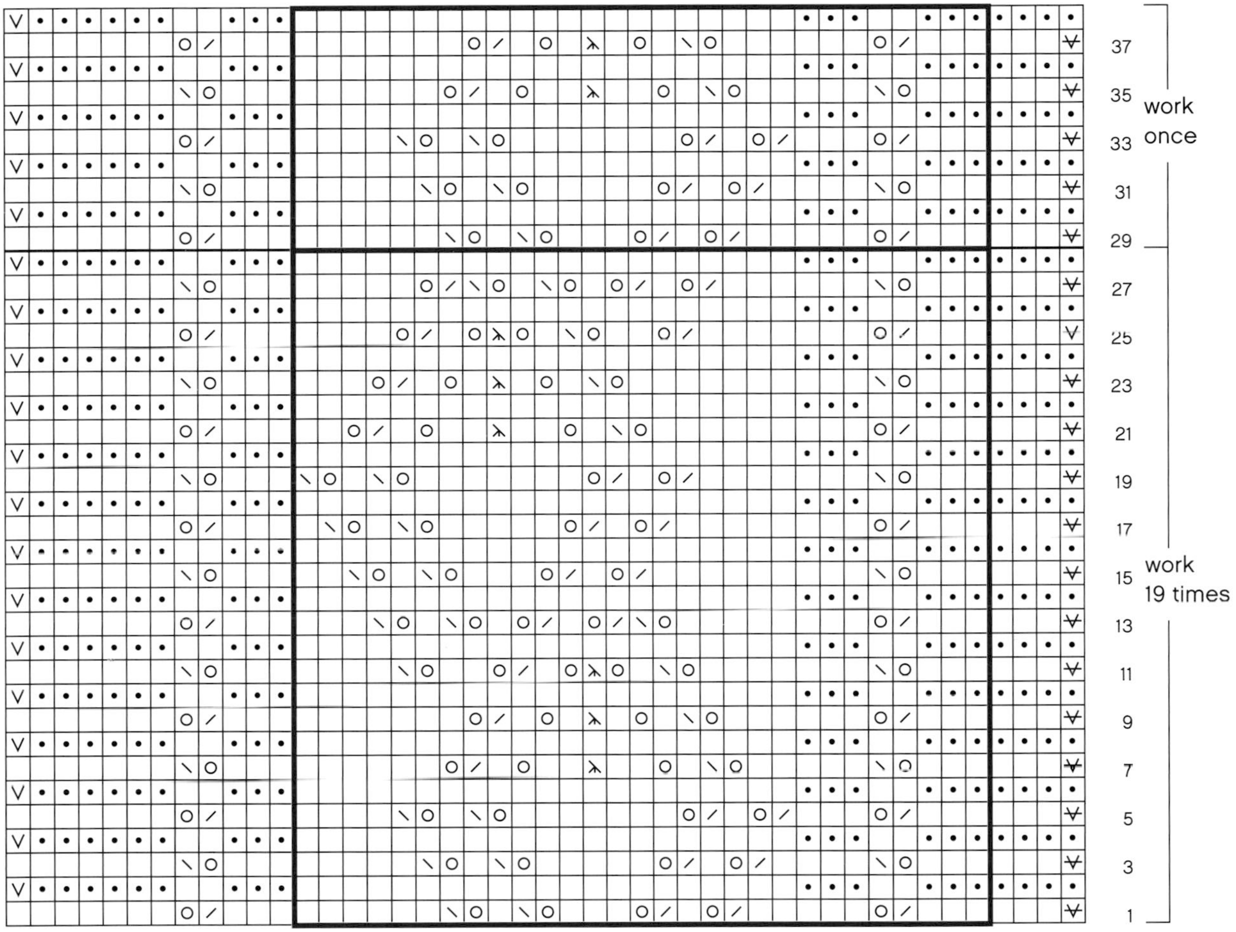

work once

work 19 times

37
35
33
31
29
27
25
23
21
19
17
15
13
11
9
7
5
3
1

29-st repeat, work twice

	knit on RS; purl on WS	/	k2tog	⅄	sl 1 pwise wyf on RS
•	purl on RS; knit on WS	\	ssk	V	sl 1 pwise wyf on WS
O	yo	⅄	sl 1, k2tog, psso	☐	pattern repeat

Winter Garden Wrap

DESIGNED BY
ROSEMARY (ROMI) HILL

Inspired by vintage square doilies, the center section of **Romi Hill's** generous wrap begins at the center and is worked outward in rounds to form an expanding square. The stitches are bound off along two sides of the square, then each "tail" is worked outward in rows in a lacy leaf pattern that ends in a pretty scallop at the bind-off edge. Romi chose a lightly spun singles yarn in a luxurious blend of extra-fine merino and cashmere, then blocked the piece a bit aggressively to display the openwork pattern to its best effect.

FINISHED SIZE

About 17¾" (45 cm) wide and 66" (167.5 cm) long.

YARN

Worsted weight (#4 Medium).

Shown here: Debbie Macomber Blossom Street Collection Cashmere Fleur De Lys (90% extrafine merino, 10% cashmere; 93 yd [85 m]/50 g): #402 ennui (gray), 8 skeins.

NEEDLES

Start of center motif: size U.S. 6 (4 mm): set of 4 or 5 double-pointed (dpn).

Body: size U.S. 8 (5 mm): 16" and 24" (40 and 60 cm) circular (cir) and set of 4 or 5 dpn.

Adjust needle size if necessary to obtain the correct gauge.

NOTIONS

Markers (m); tapestry needle; blocking wires and T-pins.

GAUGE

14 sts and 24 rows = 4" (10 cm) in fill stitch patt (see Stitch Guide) on larger needles.

design techniques

Combined lace patterns, page 149.

Flat rectangle worked from center medallion to tails, page 144.

Circular cast-on at center, page 164.

Yarnover increases, page 168.

Garter-stitch borders, page 154.

Stretchy lace bind-off, at right.

stitch guide

Fill Stitch
(multiple of 4 sts + 1; used for swatching)

Row 1: (RS) K1, *p1, k1; rep from *.

Row 2: (WS) P1, *k1, p1; rep from *.

Row 3: P1, *k3, p1; rep from *.

Row 4: K1, *p3, k1; rep from *.

Rows 5 and 6: Rep Rows 1 and 2.

Row 7: K2, *p1, k3; rep from * to last 3 sts, p1, k2.

Row 8: P2, *k1, p3; rep from * to last 3 sts, k1, p2.

Rep Rows 1–8 for patt.

5-st Nupp: With RS facing, very loosely work ([k1, yo] 2 times, k1) all in same st—5 sts made from 1 st. On the foll rnd, knit these 5 sts tog to dec them back to 1 st.

RS Stretchy Lace Bind-Off: P2, return these 2 sts to left needle tip, k2tog through back loop (tbl)—1 st BO; 1 st on right needle. *P1, return 2 sts to left needle tip, k2tog tbl; rep from * until the desired number of sts has been BO—1 st rem on right needle after last BO.

WS Stretchy Lace Bind-Off: K2, return these 2 sts to left needle tip, k2tog through back loop (tbl)—1 st BO; 1 st on right needle. *K1, return 2 sts to left needle tip, k2tog tbl; rep from * until the desired number of sts has been BO—1 st rem on right needle after last BO.

notes

○ The gauge of this project is deliberately looser than typical for worsted-weight yarn to create a softly draping fabric.

○ Charts A and B are worked in rounds; Charts C, D, E, and F are worked in rows.

○ As you increase for the center section, change from double-pointed needles to progressively longer circular needles as necessary to accommodate the growing number of stitches.

○ The stitch count for Chart E does not remain constant throughout. It begins with a total of 69 stitches. The center 37 stitches gradually decrease to a minimum of 29 stitches, then increase to 37 stitches again, so that the chart ends with a total of 69 stitches.

○ This project features two left-leaning double decreases (sl 1, k2tog, psso and sssk), and uses their different appearances to enhance the lace patterns.

Wrap

Center

With smaller dpns and using Emily Ocker's method (see Glossary), CO 8 sts. Place marker (pm) and join for working in rnds.

Work Rnds 1–10 of Chart A, working patt rep 4 times in each rnd—32 sts.

Change to larger dpns.

Work Rnds 11–31 of Chart A, changing to cir needle as necessary (see Notes)—100 sts.

Chart A

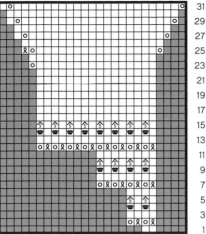

2-st repeat
inc'd to 25-st repeat

Chart B

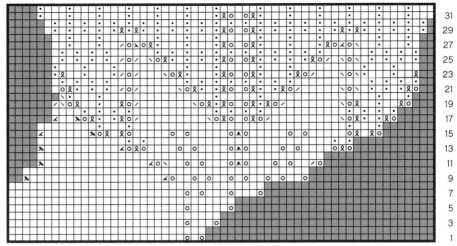

25-st repeat
inc'd to 54-st repeat

☐	k on RS rows and all rnds; p on WS rows
•	p on RS rows and all rnds; k on WS rows
ℓ	k1tbl on RS rows and all rnds; p1tbl on WS rows
ℓ	k1tbl on WS rows and all rnds; p1tbl on RS rows
O	yo
/	k2tog
\	ssk
⅄	k3tog
⅄	sl 1, k2tog, psso
⩘	sssk
∧	sl 2 as if to k2tog, k1, p2sso
♛	5-st nupp (see Stitch Guide)
⌃	k5tog
▨	no stitch
☐	pattern repeat

Next rnd: Knit to last st, temporarily sl last st to right needle tip, remove m, return slipped st to left needle tip, and replace m—end-of-rnd m has moved 1 st to the right.

Work Rnds 1–32 of Chart B, working patt rep 4 times in each rnd—216 sts.

Transition for Working Tails

Cut yarn. Without working any sts, slip the last 26 sts just worked from right needle tip to left needle tip, then rejoin yarn to beg of slipped sts with RS facing.

Next row: Use the RS stretchy lace method (see Stitch Guide) to BO 51 sts, then work Row 1 of Chart C (see page 95) over 57 sts (the st on right needle after BO counts as first st of Chart C)—57 sts on right needle. Place these 57 sts on spare needle or holder to work later—108 center section sts rem on needle.

With RS of center still facing, use the RS stretchy lace method to BO 51 sts, then work Row 1 of Chart C over 57 sts (the st on right needle after BO counts as the first st of Chart C)—57 sts rem.

First Tail

Working back and forth in rows on 57 sts, work Rows 2–16 of Chart C.

Next row: (RS) Establish patt from Row 1 of Chart D as foll: Work first 4 sts once, work first 4-st patt rep box 3 times, work center 25 sts once while inc them to 27 sts as shown, work second 4-st patt rep box 3 times, work last 4 sts once—59 sts.

Work Rows 2–16 of Chart D, working incs in center as shown—69 sts.

Next row: (RS) Establish patt from Row 1 of Chart E as foll: Work first 4 sts once, work first 4-st patt rep box 3 times, work center 37 sts once while dec them to 35 sts as shown, work second 4-st patt rep box 3 times, work last 4 sts once—67 sts.

Work Rows 2–16 of Chart E once (see Notes).

Work Rows 1–16 of Chart E 5 more times—69 sts; 96 total rows for Chart E.

Next row: (RS) Establish patt from Row 1 of Chart F as foll: Work first 4 sts once, work first 4-st patt rep box 3 times, work center 37 sts once, work second 4-st patt rep box 3 times, work last 4 sts once.

Work Rows 2–17 of Chart F once, ending with a RS row.

Use the WS stretchy lace method (see Stitch Guide) to BO all sts.

Second Tail

Return 57 held sts to larger cir needle and rejoin yarn with WS facing.

Beg with WS Row 2 of Chart C, complete as for first tail.

Finishing

Weave in loose ends.

Soak in wool wash and squeeze out excess moisture. Place on clean flat surface and insert blocking wires through edge sts. Use T-pins to pin wires to measurements, pinning out ends of leaves and petals in center motif, and scallops at ends of tails. Allow to air-dry thoroughly before removing wires and pins.

Chart C

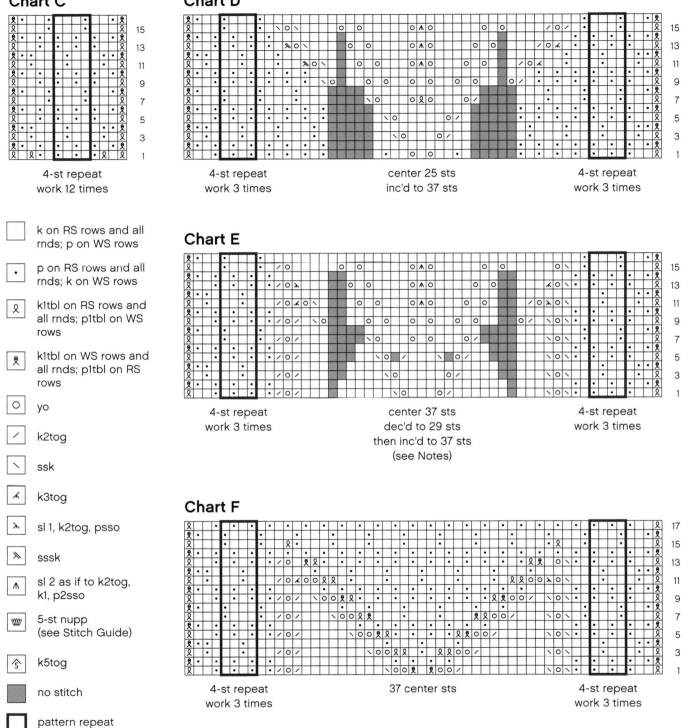

4-st repeat
work 12 times

Chart D

4-st repeat
work 3 times

center 25 sts
inc'd to 37 sts

4-st repeat
work 3 times

Chart E

4-st repeat
work 3 times

center 37 sts
dec'd to 29 sts
then inc'd to 37 sts
(see Notes)

4-st repeat
work 3 times

Chart F

4-st repeat
work 3 times

37 center sts

4-st repeat
work 3 times

k on RS rows and all
rnds; p on WS rows

p on RS rows and all
rnds; k on WS rows

k1tbl on RS rows and
all rnds; p1tbl on WS
rows

k1tbl on WS rows and
all rnds; p1tbl on RS
rows

O yo

／ k2tog

＼ ssk

⋏ k3tog

⋌ sl 1, k2tog, psso

⋊ sssk

∧ sl 2 as if to k2tog,
k1, p2sso

5-st nupp
(see Stitch Guide)

k5tog

no stitch

pattern repeat

Textured Cables

DESIGNED BY KATYA WILSHER

For a reversible pattern, **Katya Wilsher** combined knit-one-purl-one ribs and garter stitch in a cable pattern that looks the same on both sides of the fabric. Knitted in the round on size U.S. 10 (6 mm) needles and worked in an easy-to-memorize pattern, this chunky piece knits up quickly but offers plenty of interest along the way. Katya provided two sizes—knit one to hug your neck and another to hug your shoulders. Whichever size you choose, you can customize the width by adding or subtracting eight-stitch pattern repeats.

FINISHED SIZE

About 21 (42)" (53.5 [106.5] cm) in circumference and 12" (30.5 cm) high.

Copper cowl shown measures 21" (53.5 cm); teal cowl measures 42" (106.5 cm).

YARN

Chunky weight (#5 Bulky).

Shown here:
Small cowl: Misti Alpaca Chunky (100% baby alpaca; 109 yd [100 m]/100 g): #M707 copper melange, 3 skeins.

Large cowl: Cascade Yarns Eco+ (100% Peruvian wool, 478 yd [437 m]/250 g): #9451 Lake Chelan heather (teal), 2 skeins.

NEEDLES

Size U.S. 10 (6 mm): 16 (32)" (40 [80] cm) circular (cir) needle.

Adjust needle size if necessary to obtain the correct gauge.

NOTIONS

Marker (m); cable needle (cn); tapestry needle.

GAUGE

24½ sts and 24 rnds = 4" (10 cm) in reversible cable patt worked in rnds.

design techniques

Reversible cable pattern, page 148.

Short tube worked from the bottom up, page 145.

notes

○ The numbers for the smaller cowl are given first, followed by the numbers for the larger cowl in parentheses. If only one number or measurement is given, it applies to both versions.

○ Gauge is not critical for this project, but keep in mind that if you do work to a different gauge, the yarn amounts and finished measurements of your cowl will be different from what is given in the directions.

○ To make a wider or narrower cowl, add or subtract eight-stitch pattern repeats; each repeat added or removed will reduce or enlarge the circumference by about 1¼" (3.2 cm).

○ In the Reversible Cable chart, there is a cable worked over the last four stitches of Rnd 16 and the first four stitches of Rnd 17; work these rounds as follows:

• **Rnd 16:** Knit the first 4 sts of the rnd as shown, work in chart patt to 4 sts before end-of-rnd marker (m), sl 4 sts onto cable needle (cn) and hold in front, temporarily remove m, knit the next 4 sts indicated by the half-cable symbol, replace the end-of-rnd m.

• **Rnd 17:** Purl 4 sts from cn (indicated by the half-cable symbol) for the first 4 sts of the rnd, then work in patt to end-of-rnd m.

Cowl

CO 128 (256) sts. Place marker (pm) and join for working in rnds, being careful not to twist sts.

Set-up rnd: *P4, k4; rep from *.

Work Rnds 1–20 of Reversible Cable chart (see Notes) 3 times, then work Rnds 1–11 once more—72 rnds total, including set-up rnd; piece measures about 12" (30.5 cm) from CO. BO all sts.

Finishing

Weave in loose ends. Block to measurements.

Reversible Cable

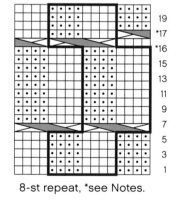

8-st repeat, *see Notes.

| | knit | · | purl | ▢ | pattern repeat |

 sl 4 sts to cn and hold in front, k4, p4 from cn

cable at end of Rnd 16 and beg of Rnd 17 (see Notes)

Shadow Play

DESIGNED BY MELISSA WEHRLE

Melissa Wehrle worked horizontal tucks along a center panel to create this three-dimensional rectangular scarf in which alternating bands of fingering and laceweight yarn provide an interesting play of color and density. Although the tucks take a little bit of concentration, the pick-up rows coincide with the boundaries between the two yarns and are therefore easy to spot. Worked in needles larger than typical for the yarn weight, this scarf has an open, ruffly appearance that works up quickly. Instead of joining new yarn for each horizontal band, floats are simply carried up along the slip-stitch selvedge.

FINISHED SIZE

About 9" (23 cm) wide and 66" (167.5 cm) long.

YARN

Fingering weight and laceweight (#1 Super Fine and #0 Lace).

Shown here: Hand Maiden Mini Maiden (50% silk, 50% wool; 547 yd [500 m]/100 g): plum (A), 1 skein.

Hand Maiden Lace Silk (100% silk; 984 yd [900 m]/100 g): plum (B), 1 skein.

NEEDLES

Size U.S. 7 (4.5 mm).

Adjust needle size if necessary to obtain the correct gauge.

NOTIONS

Markers (m); tapestry needle.

GAUGE

22 sts and 40 rows = 4" (10 cm) in St st, worked in stripes of *4 rows A, 6 rows B; rep from *.

40 rows (four 10-row repeats) of tucked section measure about 3" (7.5 cm) high.

design techniques

Stockinette-stitch with tucks, page 150.

Flat rectangle worked from tail to tail, page 144.

Stripes of two weights of yarn, page 151.

Narrow I-cord edging worked simultaneously with scarf, see below.

stitch guide

Edging Pattern
(worked over 4 sts at each end of row)

> **RS rows:** Work first 4 sts as [k1, sl 1 purlwise with yarn in front (pwise wyf)] 2 times, work in patt to last 4 sts, work last 4 sts as [sl 1 pwise wyf, k1] 2 times.
>
> **WS rows:** Work first 4 sts as [sl 1 pwise wyf, k1] 2 times, work in patt to last 4 sts, work last 4 sts as [k1, sl 1 pwise wyf] 2 times.
>
> Rep these 2 rows for patt.

notes

○ The needles used for this project are deliberately larger than typical for fingering or laceweight yarns to create an open, lacy fabric with a loose gauge.

○ Carry the yarn not in use along the selvedge at the beginning of RS rows to avoid having ends to weave in later.

○ When changing yarns, stretch the piece vertically so the tension remains the same at both selvedges, taking care that the edge with the carried yarn is not puckered.

Scarf

With A, CO 47 sts.

Set-up row: (WS) With A, work 4 sts in edging patt (see Stitch Guide), p13, place marker (pm), p13, pm, p13, work 4 sts in edging patt.

Keeping the 4 sts at each end of row in established edging patt, work rem sts as foll:

Rows 1 (RS)–4 (WS): With A, work 4 rows in St st (knit RS rows; purl WS rows).

Rows 5–10: With B, work 6 rows in St st.

Row 11: (RS; tuck row) With A, knit to marked center section, slip marker (sl m), *identify the st in Row 5 that is directly below the next st on the left needle (this will be a st in the first row of the 6-row B stripe), insert right needle tip into the WS purl bump of this st and lift it onto the left needle, then work the next st and the lifted bump tog as k2tog; rep from * 12 more times, sl m, knit to end of row.

Rows 12–14: With A, work 3 rows in St st.

Rows 15–20: With B, work 6 rows in St st.

Rep Rows 11–20 until piece measures about 65½" (166.5 cm) from CO edge measured up the center of the tucked section, then work Row 11 once more, ending with a RS tuck row.

Note: *Scarf shown has a total of 87 tucks.*

With A and keeping edge sts as established, work 4 rows in St st, ending with a RS row—piece measures about 66" (167.5 cm) from CO.

With A, loosely BO all sts.

Finishing

Block to measurements. Weave in loose ends.

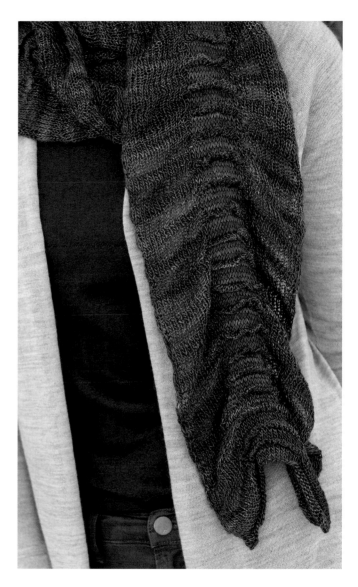

Cable-Edged Shawlette

DESIGNED BY CONNIE CHANG CHINCHIO

Connie Chang Chinchio is a great fan of small shawls knitted in sock-weight yarn. Not only do they result in beautiful and economic little works of art, but Connie typically doesn't have to look beyond her own stash for a suitable ball of yarn. She added a literal twist to this shawl's airiness by edging the simple star mesh pattern with a more substantial reversible cable border. By working increases at a faster rate along the edges than along the center back, Connie made the tails curve in gentle arcs that help the shawl stay in place.

FINISHED SIZE
About 36" (91.5 cm) measured along curved top edge and 16¼" (41.5 cm) long from center of top edge to bottom point, after blocking.

YARN
Fingering weight (#1 Super Fine).

Shown here: Malabrigo Sock (100% superwash merino; 440 yd [402 m]/100 g): #806 impressionist sky, 1 skein.

NEEDLES
Size U.S. 5 (3.75 mm).

Adjust needle size if necessary to obtain the correct gauge.

NOTIONS
Markers (m); cable needle (cn); tapestry needle.

GAUGE
23 sts and 32 rows = 4" (10 cm) in lace pattern, after blocking.

design techniques

Combined lace and reversible cables, page 152.

Triangle worked from top to bottom and shaped with
increases, page 147.

Make-One (M1) increases, page 168.

Garter-stitch and reversible cable edgings,
pages 154 and 155.

stitch guide

7/8LC: Sl 7 sts onto cn and hold in front, [k1, p1] 4 times,
then work [k1, p1] 3 times, k1 from cn.

7/8RC: Sl 8 sts onto cn and hold in back, [k1, p1] 3
times, k1, then work [p1, k1] 4 times from cn.

Left Rib Cable (worked over 15 sts)

Row 1: (RS) [K1, p1] 7 times, k1.

Row 2: (WS) [P1, k1] 7 times, p1.

Rows 3–6: Rep Rows 1 and 2 two times.

Row 7: Work 7/8LC (see at left).

Row 8: (WS) Rep Row 2.

Rows 9–12: Rep Rows 1 and 2 two times.

Rep Rows 1–12 for patt.

Right Rib Cable (worked over 15 sts)

Row 1: (RS) [K1, p1] 7 times, k1.

Row 2: (WS) [P1, k1] 7 times, p1.

Rows 3–6: Rep Rows 1 and 2 two times.

Row 7: Work 7/8RC (see at left).

Row 8: (WS) Rep Row 2.

Rows 9–12: Rep Rows 1 and 2 two times.

Rep Rows 1–12 for patt.

Shawl

CO 9 sts.

Center Back Neck

Set-up row: (WS) P1, k1, p1, place marker (pm), p1, k1, p1,
pm, p1, k1, p1.

Slipping markers (sl m) every row as you come to them,
work either Rows 1–16 of Center Back chart (placing new
m in Row 13 as shown on page 108) or work written instructions for Rows 1–16 as foll:

Row 1: (RS) K1, p1, k1, M1 (see Glossary), slip marker (sl m),
M1, k1, p1, k1, M1, sl m, M1, k1, p1, k1—4 sts inc'd total;
2 sts inc'd in center section between m; 1 st inc'd outside
m at each side.

Row 2: (WS) Working new sts into k1, p1 patt, work sts as
they appear (knit the knits and purl the purls) to m, M1,
sl m, work sts as they appear to next m, sl m, M1, work sts
as they appear to end—2 sts inc'd total; 1 st inc'd outside
m at each side.

Row 3: *Work in established rib patt to m, M1, sl m, M1;
rep from * once more, work in established rib patt to
end—4 sts inc'd total; 2 sts inc'd in center section; 1 st
inc'd outside m at each side.

Row 4: Work in established rib patt to m, M1, sl m, work center section as established to m, sl m, M1, work in established rib patt to end—2 sts inc'd total; 1 st inc'd outside m at each side.

Rows 5–12: Rep Rows 3 and 4 four times—45 sts; 3 marked sections of 15 sts each.

Row 13: Work 15 sts in established rib patt, sl m, M1, place new marker, work 15 sts in established rib patt, place new marker, M1, sl m, work 15 sts in established rib patt—2 sts inc'd total; 1 st inc'd in each new section on each side of center 15 sts.

Row 14: Work 15 sts in rib patt, sl m, M1, p1, sl m, work 15 sts in rib patt, sl m, p1, M1, sl m, work 15 sts in rib patt—2 sts inc'd total; 1 st inc'd in each section on each side of center.

Row 15: Work 15 sts in rib patt, sl m, M1, k2, M1, sl m, work 15 sts in rib patt, sl m, M1, k2, M1, sl m, work 15 sts in rib patt—4 sts inc'd total; 2 sts inc'd in each section on each side of center.

Row 16: Work 15 sts in rib patt, sl m, M1, p4, sl m, work 15 sts in rib patt, sl m, p4, M1, sl m, work 15 sts in rib patt—55 sts total; 15 center sts; 5 St sts in marked sections on each side of center; 15 sts outside markers at each end of row.

Body

Work according to chart or words as foll.

Charted Pattern

Note: *Repeat Rows 1–8 for the lace sections of the chart and rep Rows 1–12 for the cable sections. You may find it helpful to use two row counters or another method to keep track of the patts separately.*

Note: *The first time you work the chart, there will only be enough sts to work each red outlined 4-st lace rep once. Each time you rep Rows 1–8 of the charted lace sections, 12 new sts will be inc'd in each section. This will be enough new sts to work each red outlined patt rep 3 additional times on the next 8-row rep. For example, there will be 17 sts in each lace section after completing Rows 1–8 the first time. When you begin the pattern again with Row 1, there will be enough sts to work each red rep box 4 times. The next time you begin the patt again with Row 1, there will be enough sts to work each red rep box 7 times, and so on.*

Establish Body chart (see page 108) as foll:

Next row: (RS; Row 1 of chart) Work 15 cable sts, sl m, work 5 lace sts and inc them to 7 sts as shown, sl m, work 15 cable sts, sl m, work 5 lace sts and inc them to 7 sts as shown, sl m, work 15 cable sts to end—4 sts inc'd total; 2 sts inc'd in each lace section.

Cont in patt from Body chart, work 106 more rows (107 rows total for this chart), ending with Row 3 of lace patts and Row 11 of cable patts—377 sts total; 166 sts in each lace section; three 15-st cable sections.

Written Pattern

Note: *The lace patt with incs is worked over 8 rows at the same time as the cables are worked over 12 rows. Both patts begin with Row 1, then the lace patt reps Rows 1–8 as given below while the cable patt reps Rows 1–12 as given in the Stitch Guide. You may find it helpful to use two row counters or another method to keep track of the patterns separately.*

Work the lace patt with incs at the same time as cable patts as foll:

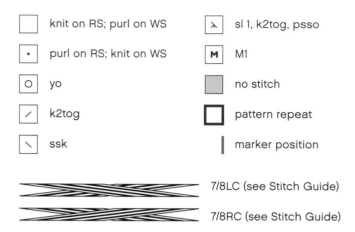

☐ knit on RS; purl on WS	⅄ sl 1, k2tog, psso
· purl on RS; knit on WS	M M1
○ yo	▨ no stitch
╱ k2tog	☐ pattern repeat
╲ ssk	│ marker position

7/8LC (see Stitch Guide)

7/8RC (see Stitch Guide)

Row 1: (RS) Work left rib cable patt (see Stitch Guide) over 15 sts, sl m, M1, *k1, yo, sl 1, k2tog, psso, yo; rep from * to 1 st before m, k1, M1, sl m, work left rib cable patt over 15 sts, sl m, M1, k1, **yo, sl 1, k2tog, psso, yo, k1; rep from ** to next m, M1, sl m, work right rib cable patt (see Stitch Guide) over 15 sts—4 sts inc'd total; 2 sts inc'd in each lace section.

Row 2: (WS) Work 15 sts in cable patt, sl m, M1, purl to next m, sl m, work 15 sts cable patt, sl m, purl to next m, M1, sl m, work 15 sts in cable patt—2 sts inc'd total; 1 st inc'd in each lace section.

Row 3: Work 15 sts in cable patt, sl m, M1, k1, *yo, sl 1, k2tog, psso, yo, k1; rep from * to 3 sts before next m, yo, ssk, k1, M1, sl m, work 15 sts in cable patt, sl m, M1, k1, k2tog, yo, **k1, yo, sl 1, k2tog, psso, yo; rep from ** to 1 st before next m, k1, M1, sl m, work 15 sts in cable patt—4 sts inc'd total; 2 sts inc'd in each lace section.

Center Back

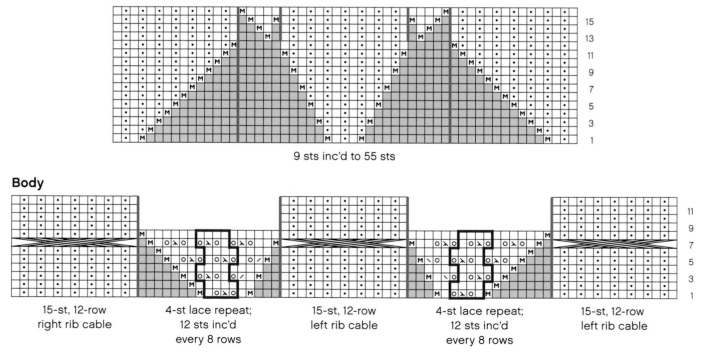

9 sts inc'd to 55 sts

Body

15-st, 12-row right rib cable

4-st lace repeat; 12 sts inc'd every 8 rows

15-st, 12-row left rib cable

4-st lace repeat; 12 sts inc'd every 8 rows

15-st, 12-row left rib cable

Row 4: Rep Row 2—2 sts inc'd total; 1 st inc'd in each lace section.

Row 5: Work 15 sts in cable patt, sl m, M1, *k1, yo, sl 1, k2tog, psso, yo; rep from * to 3 sts before next m, k1, yo, ssk, M1, sl m, work 15 sts in cable patt, sl m, M1, k2tog, yo, k1, **yo, sl 1, k2tog, psso, yo, k1; rep from ** to next m, M1, sl m, work 15 sts in cable patt—4 sts inc'd total; 2 sts inc'd in each lace section.

Row 6: Rep Row 2—2 sts inc'd total; 1 st inc'd in each lace section.

Row 7: Work 15 sts in cable patt, sl m, M1, k1, *yo, sl 1, k2tog, psso, yo, k1; rep from * to 5 sts before next m, yo, sl 1, k2tog, psso, yo, k2, M1, sl m, work 15 sts in cable patt, sl m, M1, k2, yo, sl 1, k2tog, psso, yo, **k1, yo, sl 1, k2tog, psso, yo; rep from ** to 1 st before next m, k1, M1, sl m, work 15 sts in cable patt—4 sts inc'd total; 2 sts inc'd in each lace section.

Row 8: Rep Row 2—2 sts inc'd total; 1 st inc'd in each lace section.

Cont working cable patts as established, work Rows 1–8 of lace patt with incs 12 more times, then work Rows 1–3 once more (107 rows total), ending with a RS lace row and Row 11 of cable patts—377 sts total; 166 sts in each lace section; three 15-st cable sections.

Garter Edging

Note: *The cable patterns continue to the end of the shawl while the stitches of the lace section are worked in garter stitch.*

Row 1: (WS) Work 15 sts in cable patt m, sl m, M1, knit to m, sl m, work 15 sts in cable patt, sl m, knit to m, M1, sl m, work 15 sts in cable patt—2 sts inc'd total; 1 st inc'd in each former lace section.

Row 2: (RS) *Work 15 sts in cable patt, sl m, M1, knit to m, M1, sl m; rep from * once more, work 15 sts in cable patt—4 sts inc'd total; 2 sts inc'd in each former lace section.

Rep Rows 1 and 2 two more times, ending with Row 5 of cable patts—395 sts total; 175 sts in each former lace section; three 15-st cables.

With WS facing, BO all sts knitwise.

Finishing

Weave in loose ends. Block to measurements.

Ilme's Autumn Triangle

DESIGNED BY
NANCY BUSH

An expert on Estonian knitting, **Nancy Bush** modeled this shawl after the small triangular scarves currently made along the west coast in the vicinity of Haapsalu. While early scarves from the area were typically square or rectangular, small triangular scarves that just covered the shoulders became popular in the 1930s. Worked from the point up to the top edge, Nancy's version incorporates classic patterns, including a scalloped outer edge, a wide openwork border, and a smaller openwork pattern for the center, divided by garter-stitch bands that feature small "gathered" stitches.

FINISHED SIZE
About 54" (137 cm) wide across top edge and 36" (91.5 cm) long from center of top edge to bottom point, after blocking.

YARN
Laceweight (#0 Lace).

Shown here: Elemental Affects Shetland Rustic Lace (100% North American Shetland wool; 660 yd [600 m]/100 g): #016 bronze, 2 skeins.

NEEDLES
Size U.S. 4 (3.5 mm): 32" (80 cm) or longer circular (cir) and 2 double-pointed (dpn) for Kitchener st or three-needle bind-off.

Adjust needle size if necessary to obtain the correct gauge.

NOTIONS
Markers (m); tapestry needle; coil-less safety pin or removable marker; blocking wires and T-pins.

GAUGE
20 sts and 32 rows = 4" (10 cm) in St st, before blocking.

17 sts and 28 rows = 4" (10 cm) in allover lace patt from Top charts, after blocking.

design techniques

Combined lace patterns, page 149.

Triangle worked from bottom to top and shaped with decreases, page 146.

Knitted cast-on with two strands held together, page 165.

Mirrored decreases, page 158.

Garter-stitch edging at long top edge, page 154.

Kitchener stitch finish, page 169.

stitch guide

Slipped Selvedge Sts: On both RS and WS, slip the first st as if to purl with yarn in front (pwise wyf), then bring the yarn to the back of the work between the needles.

5-st Nupp: With RS facing, very loosely work [k1, yo, k1, yo, k1] all in same st—5 sts made from 1 st. On the foll WS row, purl these 5 sts tog to dec them back to 1 st.

Gathered Sts: (worked over 3 sts) K3tog but do not slip sts from needle, yo, then knit the same 3 sts tog again, then sl all 3 sts from needle tog—3 sts made from 3 sts.

Shawl

With two strands of yarn held tog, use the knitted method (see Glossary) to CO 351 sts. Drop one strand and continue with a single strand of yarn throughout.

Knit 2 rows, ending with a WS row.

Lower Edge Pattern

Establish patts from Row 1 of both Right Lower Edge and Left Lower Edge charts as foll: (RS) Work first 4 sts of Right Lower Edge chart, place marker (pm), work next 19 sts and dec them to 18 sts as shown, work 16-st patt rep 8 times, work next 24 sts of chart, k1 for last st of chart (center st) and place a coil-less safety pin or removable marker in center st; work the first 25 sts of Left Lower Edge chart, work the 16-st patt rep 8 times, work next 18 sts of chart and dec them to 17 sts as shown, pm, work last 4 sts of chart—349 sts rem; 1 marked center st; 170 patt sts and 4 border sts at each side.

Note: *Move the marker in the center st up as the work progresses so you can easily identify the center st.*

Work Rows 2–25 of charts, ending with a RS row—313 sts rem; 1 marked center st; 148 patt sts and 8 border sts at each side.

First Gathered Stitches Pattern

Rows 1 and 3: (WS) Sl 1 pwise wyf, k7, slip marker (sl m), knit to last 8 sts, sl m, k8.

Rows 2 and 4: (RS) Sl 1 pwise wyf, k7, sl m, [sl 1, k1, psso], knit to 1 st before center st, [sl 1, k2tog, psso], knit to 2 sts before next m, k2tog, sl m, k8—4 sts dec'd each row; 305 sts after Row 4; 1 marked center st; 144 patt sts and 8 border sts at each side.

Row 5: Sl 1 pwise wyf, k7, sl m, purl to last 8 sts, sl m, k8.

Row 6: (RS; gathered sts row) Sl 1 pwise wyf, k7, sl m, sl 1, k1, psso, [work gathered sts (see Stitch Guide) over 3 sts] 47 times to 1 st before center st, sl 1, k2tog, psso, [work gathered st over 3 sts] 47 times, k2tog, sl m, k8—4 sts dec'd.

Left Lower Edge

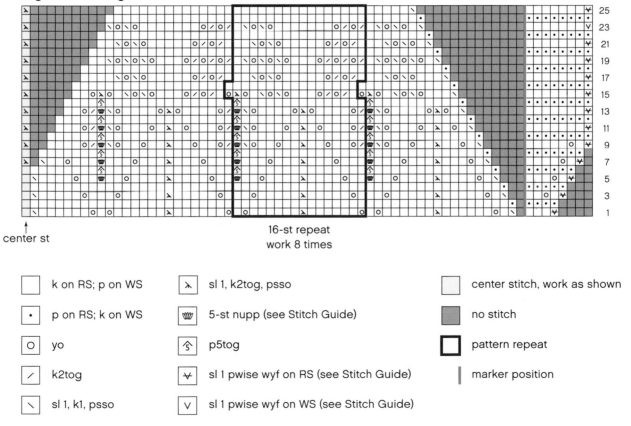

16-st repeat
work 8 times

Right Lower Edge

16-st repeat
work 8 times

center st

	k on RS; p on WS		sl 1, k2tog, psso		center stitch, work as shown
•	p on RS; k on WS	5-st nupp (see Stitch Guide)			no stitch
O	yo		p5tog		pattern repeat
╱	k2tog		sl 1 pwise wyf on RS (see Stitch Guide)		marker position
╲	sl 1, k1, psso		sl 1 pwise wyf on WS (see Stitch Guide)		

Row 7: Rep Row 5.

Rows 8 and 10: Rep Row 2—4 sts dec'd each row.

Rows 9 and 11: Rep Row 1.

Row 12: Rep Row 2—4 sts dec'd; 289 sts rem; 1 marked center st; 136 patt sts and 8 border sts at each side.

Row 13: Rep Row 5.

Diamond Border Pattern

Establish patts from Row 1 of both Right Diamond Border and Left Diamond Border charts (see pages 116 and 117) as foll: (RS) Work first 8 sts of Right Diamond Border chart, sl m, work next 24 sts of chart dec them to 23 sts as shown, work 16-st patt rep 6 times, work next 15 sts of chart to 1 st before marked center st, work [sl 1, k2tog, psso] in next 3 sts as shown; work the first 16 sts of Left Diamond Border chart, work the 16-st patt rep 6 times, work next 23 sts of chart dec them to 22 sts as shown, sl m, work last 8 sts of chart—285 sts rem; 1 marked center st; 134 patt sts and 8 border sts at each side.

Work Rows 2–27 of charts, ending with a RS row—233 sts rem; 1 marked center st; 108 patt sts and 8 border sts at each side.

Second Gathered Stitches Pattern

Rows 1 and 3: (WS) Sl 1 pwise wyf, k7, slip marker (sl m), knit to last 8 sts, sl m, k8.

Rows 2 and 4: (RS) Sl 1 pwise wyf, k7, sl m, sl 1, k1, psso, knit to 1 st before center st, sl 1, k2tog, psso, knit to 2 sts before next m, k2tog, sl m, k8—4 sts dec'd each row; 225 sts after Row 4; 1 marked center st; 104 patt sts and 8 border sts at each side.

Row 5: Sl 1 pwise wyf, k7, sl m, purl to last 8 sts, sl m, k8.

Row 6: (RS; gathered sts row) Sl 1 pwise wyf, k7, sl m, sl 1, k1, psso, [work gathered sts over 3 sts] 33 times to 3 sts before center st, k2, sl 1, k2tog, psso, k2, [work gathered st over 3 sts] 33 times, k2tog, sl m, k8—4 sts dec'd.

Row 7: Rep Row 5.

Rows 8 and 10: Rep Row 2—4 sts dec'd each row.

Rows 9 and 11: Rep Row 1.

Row 12: Rep Row 2—4 sts dec'd; 209 sts rem; 1 marked center st; 96 patt sts and 8 border sts at each side.

Row 13: Rep Row 5.

Top Pattern

Establish patts from Row 1 of both Right Top and Left Top charts as foll: (RS) Work first 8 sts of Right Top chart, sl m, work next 21 sts of chart and dec them to 20 sts as shown, work 6-st patt rep 9 times, work next 20 sts of chart to 1 st before marked center st, sl 1, k2tog, psso; work the first 21 sts of Left Top chart, work the 6-st patt rep 9 times, work next 20 sts of chart and dec them to 19 sts as shown, sl m, work last 8 sts of chart—205 sts rem; 1 marked center st; 94 patt sts and 8 border sts at each side.

Work Rows 2–24 of chart—161 sts rem; 1 marked center st; 72 patt sts and 8 border sts at each side.

Work Rows 1–24 of chart once more, working each 6-st patt rep 5 times—113 sts rem; 1 marked center st; 48 patt sts and 8 border sts at each side.

Work Rows 1–24 of chart once more, working each 6-st patt rep once—65 sts rem; 1 marked center st; 24 patt sts and 8 border sts at each side.

Work Rows 25–47 of chart once—19 sts rem; 1 marked center st; 1 patt st and 8 border sts at each side.

Next row: (WS) Removing markers as you come to them, sl 1 pwise wyf, k6, sl 1 kwise, k3tog, psso, k8—16 sts rem.

Cut yarn, leaving a 12" (30.5 cm) tail.

Finishing

Arrange rem 16 sts on two dpns so that there are 8 sts on each needle. Hold needles parallel with WS of shawl facing tog and RS facing out. Thread yarn tail onto tapestry needle and use the Kitchener st (see Glossary) to graft the sts tog (for an alternate finish work a three-needle bind-off to join the two sets of 8 sts).

Weave in loose ends.

Hand wash gently in mild soap and warm water. Rinse and squeeze out excess moisture.

Place damp shawl on clean, flat surface and thread a blocking wire through each stitch along the straight top edge and through each [sl 1, k2tog, psso] point along the lower edges. Stretch the shawl to measurements, using T-pins to pin the wires in place. Allow to air-dry thoroughly before removing pins.

Left Top

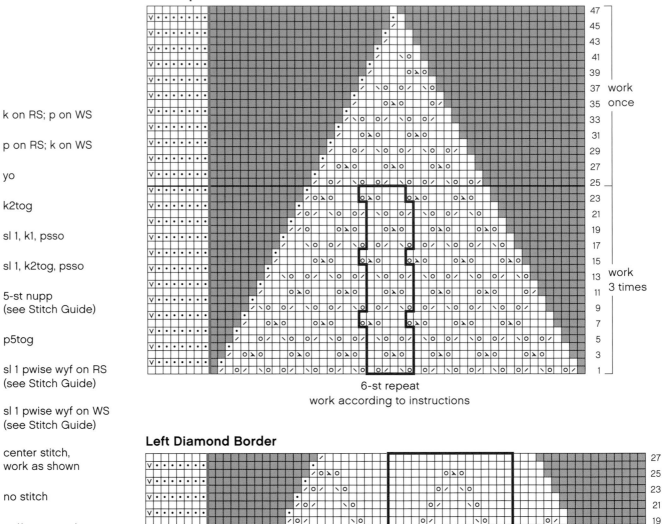

☐	k on RS; p on WS	
•	p on RS; k on WS	
O	yo	
╱	k2tog	
╲	sl 1, k1, psso	
⅄	sl 1, k2tog, psso	
♛	5-st nupp (see Stitch Guide)	
🜄	p5tog	
ⱶ	sl 1 pwise wyf on RS (see Stitch Guide)	
V	sl 1 pwise wyf on WS (see Stitch Guide)	
☐	center stitch, work as shown	
▨	no stitch	
▢	pattern repeat	
│	marker position	

Left Top row numbers (right side): 47, 45, 43, 41, 39, 37, 35, 33, 31, 29, 27, 25, 23, 21, 19, 17, 15, 13, 11, 9, 7, 5, 3, 1

work once (rows 25–47)
work 3 times (rows 1–23)

6-st repeat
work according to instructions

Left Diamond Border

row numbers (right side): 27, 25, 23, 21, 19, 17, 15, 13, 11, 9, 7, 5, 3, 1

16-st repeat
work 6 times

Right Top

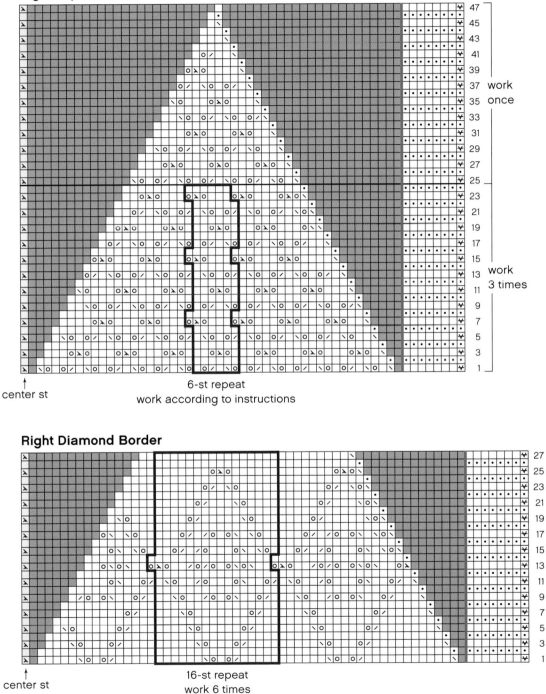

↑
center st

6-st repeat
work according to instructions

work once

work 3 times

Right Diamond Border

↑
center st

16-st repeat
work 6 times

Duplex

DESIGNED BY LAURA NELKIN

To produce a geometric shape that she calls a "fauxbius," **Laura Nelkin** started with a provisional cast-on, worked a series of short-row blocks to create a rectangle, put a half twist in the piece, then grafted the ends together to form a mobius strip. By working the short-row blocks in a combination of stockinette and garter stitch punctuated with eyelets, there is no "right" or "wrong" side. Laura finished the piece with a narrow eyelet band and used an elastic decrease bind-off to prevent the edge from drawing in.

FINISHED SIZE

About 9" (23 cm) wide, and 34 (45)" (86.5 [114.5] cm) long, after blocking and before joining ends.

Cowl shown measures 34" (86.5 cm).

YARN

Fingering weight (#1 Super Fine).

Shown here: Dream in Color Smooshy (100% merino superwash; 450 yd [411 m]/4 oz [113.5 g]): grey tabby, 1 (2) skein(s).

NEEDLES

Size U.S. 5 (3.75 mm): 40" (100 cm) or longer (to accommodate large number of sts in edging) circular (cir).

Adjust needle size if necessary to obtain the correct gauge.

NOTIONS

Size G/6 (4 mm) crochet hook and smooth waste yarn for provisional CO; spare cir needle same size or smaller than main needle for grafting; tapestry needle.

GAUGE

22 sts and 31 rows = 4" (10 cm) in St st, after blocking (see Notes).

design techniques

Reversible textured stitch patterns, page 153.

Flat rectangle joined into a twisted tube, page 146.

Provisional cast-on, page 164.

Short-row shaping, page 170.

Kitchener stitch finish, page 169.

Eyelet lace edging, page 154.

Decrease bind-off, page 161.

notes

○ The cowl and shrug are worked to different lengths on the same number of stitches. If two numbers are given, the first applies to the cowl and the second (in parentheses) applies to the shrug. If only one number is given, it applies to both versions.

○ The knit side of the stockinette blocks is referred to as the RS in the instructions to help orient the blocks correctly during knitting, but the finished piece will be completely reversible, with blocks of garter stitch, stockinette, and reverse stockinette visible when worn.

○ After blocking, each garter-stitch block measures about 5" (12.5 cm) high and each stockinette block measures about 6¼" (16 cm) high, measured straight up in the center of the block.

○ For a longer shrug, work more sets of garter and stockinette blocks; each garter/stockinette pair added will lengthen the piece by about 11¼" (28.5 cm). For a wider shrug, cast on more stitches, making sure the total is an odd number, and repeat the 2-row short-row sequences in each block until the last wrapped stitch is the second stitch from the beginning or end of the needle. Every five to six stitches added will increase the width by about 1" (2.5 cm). Plan to purchase extra yarn if making a bigger shrug.

Cowl or Shrug

With crochet hook and smooth waste yarn, use the crochet provisional method (see Glossary) to provisionally CO 45 sts.

Change to main yarn.

Garter-Stitch Block

Work garter st block using short-rows (see Glossary) as foll:

Row 1: (RS) For first block only, knit all sts; for subsequent blocks, sl first st purlwise with yarn in back (pwise wyb), knit to end.

Row 2: (WS) Knit to last 2 sts, wrap next st, turn work.

Row 3: Knit to end.

Row 4: Knit to 2 sts before previous wrapped st, wrap next st, turn work.

Rows 5–44: Rep Rows 3 and 4 twenty more times—22 wrapped sts total; with RS facing, last wrapped st is the 2nd st from the end of the row.

Row 45: Knit to end.

Row 46: Knit across all sts without working wraps tog with wrapped sts.

Row 47: Knit to end.

Row 48: (WS; eyelet row) P1, *yo, p2tog; rep from *.

Rows 49 and 50: Knit to end.

Row 51: Knit to last 2 sts, wrap next st, turn work.

Row 52: Knit to end.

Row 53: Knit to 2 sts before previous wrapped st, wrap next st, turn work.

Row 54: Knit to end.

Rows 55–94: Rep Rows 53 and 54 twenty more times—22 wrapped sts total; with RS facing, last wrapped st is the 2nd st from beg of the row.

Stockinette-Stitch Block

Work St st block using short-rows as foll:

Row 1: (RS) Knit to end without working wraps tog with wrapped sts.

Row 2: (WS) Sl 1 purlwise with yarn in front (pwise wyf), purl to end.

Row 3: Sl 1 pwise wyb, knit to last 2 sts, wrap next st, turn work.

Row 4: Purl to end.

Row 5: Sl 1 pwise wyb, knit to 2 sts before previous wrapped st, wrap next st, turn work.

Row 6: Purl to end.

Rows 7–46: Rep Rows 5 and 6 twenty more times—22 wrapped sts total; with RS facing last wrapped st is the 2nd st from beg of the row.

Row 47: Sl 1 pwise wyb, knit across all sts, working wraps tog with wrapped sts.

Row 48: Sl 1 pwise with yarn in front (wyf), purl to end.

Row 49: (RS; eyelet row) Sl 1 pwise wyb, k1, k1, *yo, k2tog; yo, k2tog; rep from * to last st, k1.

Row 50: Sl 1 pwise wyf, purl to end.

Row 51: Sl 1 pwise wyb, knit to end.

Row 52: Sl 1 pwise wyf, purl to last 2 sts, wrap next st, turn work.

Row 53: Knit to end.

Row 54: Sl 1 pwise wyf, purl to 2 sts before previous wrapped st, wrap next st, turn work.

Row 55: Knit to end.

Rows 56–95: Rep Rows 54 and 55 twenty more times—22 wrapped sts total; with RS facing, last wrapped st is the 2nd st from end of the row.

Row 96: Sl 1 pwise wyf, purl to end, working wraps tog with wrapped sts.

[Work Rows 1–92 of garter st block, then work Rows 1–96 of St st block] 2 (3) more times, omitting WS Row 96 in the final block—6 (8) blocks total; 3 (4) blocks each of alternating garter and St st.

Finishing

Carefully remove waste yarn from provisional CO and place 45 exposed sts on spare cir needle. Allow piece to dangle from needle holding live sts, flip the needle holding CO sts to put a half-twist in the piece, and bring the needles together so that they are parallel. Cut yarn, leaving a tail about three times the width of the piece. Thread tail on a tapestry needle and use the Kitchener st (see Glossary) to graft the two sets of sts tog.

Edging

Join yarn to selvedge where a garter and stockinette block meet. With RS facing, pick up and knit along the single mobius selvedge 1 st in each garter ridge for garter blocks (about 23 sts), and 7 sts for every 6 slipped selvedge st for St st blocks (about 28 sts) until you reach the point where you started—about 306 (408) sts. Place marker (pm) and join for working in rnds.

Eyelet rnd: *K2tog, yo; rep from *.

Knit 1 rnd even.

Using the decrease method (see Glossary), BO all sts. Cut yarn and pull loop of last st until tail comes free.

Weave in loose ends. Block to measurements.

Ring of Roses

DESIGNED BY EVELYN A. CLARK

Evelyn A. Clark's softly draped cowl offers an elegant way to surround yourself with a little luxury. Beginning at the neck with a scalloped leaf lace edging and ending at the shoulders with a picot bind-off, a sequence of three stitch patterns based on a ten-stitch repeat makes it easy to add or remove repeats to customize the circumference. Cleverly placed increases gradually expand the main pattern to produce flare at the lower edge. This is an excellent project for a precious single skein of luxury yarn, like the cashmere shown here.

FINISHED SIZE

About 21½" (54.5 cm) circumference at neck edge, 39" (99 cm) circumference at shoulder edge, and 11" (28 cm) long, after blocking.

YARN

Laceweight (#0 Lace).

Shown here: Jojoland Crown (100% cashmere; 440 yd [402 m]/50 g): #C241 stormy blue, 1 skein.

NEEDLES

Size U.S. 2 (2.75mm): 16" (40 cm) circular (cir).

Adjust needle size if necessary to obtain the correct gauge.

NOTIONS

Marker (m); tapestry needle.

GAUGE

26 sts and 36 rnds = 4" (10 cm) in lace patterns worked in rnds, after blocking.

design techniques

Combined lace patterns, page 149.

Short tube worked from the top down with increases, page 145.

Yarnover increases, page 168.

Picot bind-off, page 126.

stitch guide

Leaf Lace (multiple of 10 sts)

Rnd 1: Purl.

Even-numbered Rnds 2–14: Knit.

Rnd 3: *Yo, k3, sl 1, k2tog, psso, k3, yo, k1; rep from *.

Rnd 5: *K1, yo, k2, sl 1, k2tog, psso, k2, yo, k2; rep from *.

Rnd 7: *Yo, ssk, yo, k1, sl 1, k2tog, psso, k1, yo, k2tog, yo, k1; rep from *.

Rnd 9: *K1, yo, ssk, yo, sl 1, k2tog, psso, yo, k2tog, yo, k2; rep from *.

Rnds 11 and 13: *[K2tog, yo] 2 times, k1, [yo, ssk] 2 times, k1; rep from *.

Rnd 15: Remove end-of-rnd m, k1, replace m on right needle, *yo, k2tog, yo, k3, yo, ssk, yo, sl 1, k2tog, psso; rep from *.

Rnd 16: Knit.

Small Roses (multiple of 10 sts)

Rnd 1: *[K2tog, yo] 2 times, k1, [yo, ssk] 2 times, k1; rep from *.

Even-numbered Rnds 2–18: Knit.

Rnd 3: Remove end-of-rnd m, k1, replace m on right needle, *yo, k2tog, yo, k3, yo, ssk, yo, sl 1, k2tog, psso; rep from *.

Rnds 5 and 7: *[Yo, ssk] 2 times, k1, [k2tog, yo] 2 times, k1; rep from *.

Rnd 9: *K1, yo, ssk, yo, sl 1, k2tog, psso, yo, k2tog, yo, k2; rep from *.

Rnd 11: *[Yo, ssk] 2 times, k1, [k2tog, yo] 2 times, k1; rep from *.

Rnd 13: *K1, yo, ssk, yo, sl 1, k2tog, psso, yo, k2tog, yo, k2; rep from *.

Rnds 15 and 17: *[K2tog, yo] 2 times, k1, [yo, ssk] 2 times, k1; rep from *.

Rnd 19: Remove end-of-rnd m, k1, replace m on right needle, *yo, k2tog, yo, k3, yo, ssk, yo, sl 1, k2tog, psso; rep from *.

Rnd 20: Knit.

Rep Rnds 1–20 for patt.

Large Roses
(multiple of 10 sts, inc to a multiple of 18 sts)

Rnd 1: *K2tog, yo, k5, yo, ssk, k1; rep from *.

Even-numbered Rnds 2–40: Knit.

Rnd 3: Remove end-of-rnd m, k1, replace m on right needle, yo, k1, k2tog, yo, k1, yo, ssk, k1, yo, sl 1, k2tog, psso; rep from *.

Rnd 5: *Yo, k1, k2tog, yo, k3, yo, ssk, k1, yo, k1; rep from *—patt has inc'd to a multiple of 12 sts.

Rnd 7: *Yo, k1, [k2tog, yo] 2 times, k1, [yo, ssk] 2 times, k1, yo, k1; rep from *—patt has inc'd to a multiple of 14 sts.

Rnd 9: Remove end-of-rnd m, k1, replace m on right needle, *[yo, k2tog] 2 times, yo, k3, yo, [ssk, yo] 2 times, sl 1, k2tog, psso; rep from *.

Rnds 11 and 13: *[Yo, ssk] 3 times, k1, [k2tog, yo] 3 times, k1; rep from *.

Rnd 15: *Yo, ssk, k1, yo, ssk, yo, sl 1, k2tog, psso, yo, [k2tog, yo, k1] 2 times; rep from *.

Rnd 17: *[K1, yo, ssk] 2 times, [k1, k2tog, yo] 2 times, k2; rep from *.

Rnd 19: *Yo, k2, yo, ssk, k1, yo, sl 1, k2tog, psso, yo, k1, yo, k2tog, k2, yo, k1; rep from *—patt has inc'd to a multiple of 16 sts.

Rnd 21: *[K1, yo, ssk] 2 times, k3, k2tog, yo, k1, k2tog, yo, k2; rep from *.

Rnd 23: *[Yo, ssk] 2 times, k1, yo, ssk, k1, k2tog, yo, k1, [k2tog, yo] 2 times, k1; rep from *.

Rnd 25: *K1, [yo, ssk] 2 times, k1, yo, sl 1, k2tog, psso, yo, k1, [k2tog, yo] 2 times, k2; rep from *.

Rnds 27 and 29: *[K2tog, yo] 2 times, k1, k2tog, yo, k1, yo, ssk, k1, [yo, ssk] 2 times, k1; rep from *.

Rnd 31: Remove end-of-rnd m, k1, replace m on right needle, *yo, k2tog, yo, k1, k2tog, yo, k3, yo, ssk, k1, yo, ssk, yo, sl 1, k2tog, psso; rep from *.

Rnd 33: *K2tog, yo, k1, k2tog, yo, k2, yo, k1, yo, k2, [yo, ssk, k1] 2 times; rep from *—patt has inc'd to a multiple of 18 sts.

Rnd 35: Remove end-of-rnd m, k1, replace m on right needle, *yo, [k1, k2tog, yo] 2 times, k3, [yo, ssk, k1] 2 times, yo, sl 1, k2tog, psso; rep from *.

Rnd 37: *K1, k2tog, yo, k1, [k2tog, yo] 2 times, k1, [yo, ssk] 2 times, k1, yo, ssk, k2; rep from *.

Rnd 39: *K2tog, yo, k1, [k2tog, yo] 2 times, k3, [yo, ssk] 2 times, k1, yo, ssk, k1; rep from *.

Rnd 41: Remove end-of-rnd m, k1, replace m on right needle, *yo, [k1, k2tog, yo] 2 times, k3, [yo, ssk, k1] 2 times, yo, sl 1, k2tog, psso; rep from *.

Rnd 42: Knit.

Rnd 43: Purl.

notes

○ The instructions are written for a 16" (40 cm) circular needle, but you can substitute two circular needles or the magic-loop method if preferred.

○ All lace patterns are given in both charts and row-by-row instructions.

○ For the chart rounds indicated by *, the end-of-round marker is moved one stitch to the left at the beginning of the round; refer to the row-by-row instructions in the Stitch Guide for how to move the marker.

○ To make a larger or smaller cowl, cast on more or fewer stitches in groups of 10; every 10 stitches added or removed will make the cowl about 1½" (3.8 cm) larger or smaller in circumference. For a longer cowl, work the 20-round small roses pattern more times before changing to the large roses pattern; every 20 rounds added will lengthen the cowl by about 2¼" (6.5 cm). You may need more yarn if making a larger cowl.

Cowl

Loosely CO 140 sts (see Notes). Place marker (pm) and join for working in rnds, being careful not to twist sts.

Work Rnds 1–16 of Leaf Lace patt from Stitch Guide or chart.

Change to Small Roses patt from Stitch Guide or chart, and work Rnds 1–20 two times, or as desired (see Notes).

Change to Large Roses patt from Stitch Guide or chart, and work Rnds 1–43 once—252 sts after completing Rnd 33.

Finishing

Using the picot method, BO as foll: BO 1 st, *return st rem on right needle to left needle, use the knitted method (see Glossary) to CO 1 st, BO 4 sts (the new CO st and the

next 3 sts); rep from * until 1 st rem, cut yarn leaving an 8"
(20.5 cm) tail and fasten off last st. Use the yarn tail to join
the first and last sts of the BO rnd so the BO edge appears
continuous.

Weave in loose ends, but do not trim them yet.

Soak in lukewarm water for at least 20 minutes. Gently
rinse and squeeze out water. Wrap in a towel to remove
excess water. Place on clean flat surface and smooth into
shape, pulling out scallops at neck edge and picots at
shoulder edge. Allow to air-dry thoroughly before moving.

Trim ends flush with the surface of the fabric.

Large Roses

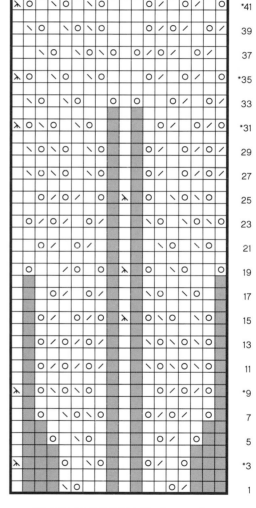

10-st repeat inc'd to 18-st repeat
*see Notes

Small Roses

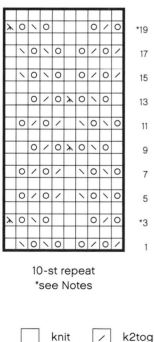

10-st repeat
*see Notes

Leaf Lace

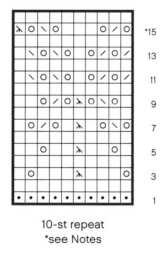

10-st repeat
*see Notes

	knit		/	k2tog			no stitch
	•	purl		\	ssk			pattern repeat
	O	yo		⅄	sl 1, k2tog, psso			

Eufaula

DESIGNED BY ALEXIS WINSLOW

Alexis Winslow designed this eternity scarf to be worn a variety of ways—as a long loop, doubled to form a cozy cowl, or with one layer pulled up over the head and worn as a hood. She chose a soft chevron stitch pattern accentuated with textural bands of garter stitch and worked it in a pure alpaca yarn for beautiful drape and excellent sheen. Worked in the round to form a continuous tube, this piece can be thrown on and twisted as desired without worrying about potential visible seams.

FINISHED SIZE

About 52" (132 cm) in circumference and 16" (40.5 cm) tall.

YARN

Worsted weight (#4 Medium).

Shown here: Blue Sky Alpacas Melange (100% baby alpaca; 110 yd [100 m]/50 g): #807 dijon (gold), 6 skeins.

NEEDLES

Size U.S. 8 (5 mm): 32" (80 cm) circular (cir) needle.

Adjust needle size if necessary to obtain the correct gauge.

NOTIONS

Markers (m; you'll need 21 plus 1 of a unique color if you place one after every patt rep); tapestry needle; blocking wires or pins.

GAUGE

18½ sts and 28 rnds = 4" (10 cm) in waves of grain patt, relaxed after blocking.

design techniques

Textured pattern stitch that forms waves at cast-on and bind-off edges, page 150.

Short tube, page 145.

Garter-stitch edging, page 154.

stitch guide

Waves of Grain (multiple of 11 sts)

Rnds 1, 3, and 5: Purl.

Rnds 2 and 4: Knit.

Rnds 6, 8, and 10: *K2tog, k2, [k1f&b (see Glossary)] 2 times, k3, ssk; rep from *.

Rnds 7, 9, and 11: Knit.

Rnd 12: Rep Rnd 6.

Rep Rnds 1–12 for patt.

notes

○ To make working the waves of grain pattern easier, place a marker after every pattern repeat.

○ The pair of k1f&b increases is intentionally not centered in the pattern repeat. This type of increase always leaves a "bar" on the left side. In this pattern, the increases are offset to account for this and will appear centered in the finished scarf.

Scarf

CO 242 sts, placing a marker after every 11 sts and using a unique color for the last marker to denote end of rnd—22 markers total. Join for working in rnds, being careful not to twist sts.

Work Rnds 1–12 of waves of grain patt from chart or Stitch Guide 9 times, then work Rnds 1–4 once more—112 rnds total; piece measures 16" (40.5 cm) from CO.

Loosely BO all sts, using a larger needle if desired.

Finishing

Weave in loose ends as invisibly as possible.

Fill a sink with water and a small amount of detergent. Submerge the scarf, letting the water soak into the fibers evenly. Rinse, being careful not to agitate the fibers. Gently squeeze out as much water as you can. Lay the scarf out on several towels or a blocking mat. Re-shape using pins or blocking wires to accentuate the chevron points of the CO and BO edges, using the finished measurements as your guide (the scarf will stretch considerably when wet, but will shrink again as it relaxes off the blocking surface). Let air-dry thoroughly before removing pins or wires.

Waves of Grain

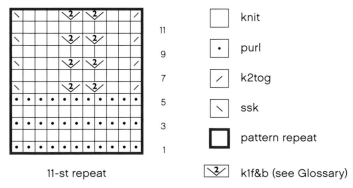

11-st repeat

	knit
	purl
∕	k2tog
＼	ssk
☐	pattern repeat
�	k1f&b (see Glossary)

Airy Lace Scarf

DESIGNED BY ANGELA TONG

To create a light and airy scarf that won't fall off the shoulders, **Angela Tong** worked a double layer of garter stitch to create a channel closure at the end of one of the tails. Slip the pointed end through the channel and pull on it to adjust the fit—wear it loosely with the ends dangling for just a bit of warmth; wrap it more tightly for greater insulation. Triangular in shape, this shawl is worked sideways from one tail to the other in a simple garter-and-eyelet pattern that requires no additional edging.

FINISHED SIZE

About 78" (198 cm) long and 13" (33 cm) wide in center, after blocking.

YARN

Laceweight (#0 Super Fine).

Shown here: Classic Elite Yarns Silky Alpaca Lace (70% baby alpaca, 30% silk; 440 yd [402 m]/50 g): #2443 apricot, 1 skein.

NEEDLES

Size U.S. 6 (4 mm): 16" (40 cm) circular (cir) and set of 3 double-pointed (dpn).

Adjust needle size if necessary to obtain the correct gauge.

NOTIONS

Tapestry needle; blocking wires and T-pins.

GAUGE

23 sts and 30 rows = 4" (10 cm) in garter and eyelet patt, after blocking (see Notes).

design techniques

Reversible garter-stitch and lace patterns, page 153.

Triangle worked side to side, page 147.

Double-layer channel for closure, at right.

Shaped along one side with bar increases, followed by right-slanting decreases, pages 156 and 158.

stitch guide

Basic Garter and Eyelet Pattern
(odd number of sts)

> **Rows 1 (RS)–12 (WS):** Work 12 rows garter st (knit every row).
>
> **Row 13:** Knit.
>
> **Row 14:** K1, purl to last st, k1.
>
> **Row 15:** K2, *yo, k2tog; rep from * to last st, k1.
>
> **Row 16:** K1, purl to last st, k1.
>
> **Rows 17–24:** Rep Rows 13–16 two times.
>
> Rep Rows 1–24 for patt.

note

○ The instructions for the garter and eyelet pattern in the body of the scarf include increases and decreases to shape the triangle. For your gauge swatch, cast on an odd number of sts and work even in the basic garter and eyelet pattern given in the Stitch Guide.

Scarf

With dpn, CO 3 sts.

Leaf Tab

Inc row: K1, k1f&b (see Glossary), knit to end—1 st inc'd.

Rep inc row 26 more times—30 sts.

Work even in garter st (knit every row) for 22 rows—leaf tab will measure about 4" (10 cm) from CO after blocking.

Double-Layer Channel

Arrange sts on 2 dpn without working them as foll: [Sl 1 st as if to purl (pwise) onto dpn held in front of work (front dpn), sl next st pwise onto second dpn held in back of work (back dpn)] 15 times—15 sts each on 2 dpn.

Slide sts on front dpn to other end of needle. Using yarn attached at beg of row, use a third dpn to work 15 sts on front dpn in garter st for 2" (5 cm), ending with a WS row. Cut yarn.

Rejoin yarn to sts on back dpn with RS facing and work as for front dpn sts, ending with a WS row. Do not cut yarn.

Joining row: Hold the 2 dpn tog in your left hand and, using the yarn attached to the back dpn, [insert the tip of the cir needle into the first st on each dpn and work them tog as k2tog] 15 times—15 sts rem on cir needle.

Increase Section

Work garter and eyelet patt while inc at beg of RS rows as foll:

Row 1: (RS) K1, k1f&b—1 st inc'd.

Rows 2–4: Knit.

Rows 5–12: Rep Rows 1–4 two times—1 st inc'd in each of Rows 5 and 9.

Row 13: K1, k1f&b, knit to end—1 st inc'd.

Row 14: K1, purl to last st, k1.

Row 15: K2, *yo, k2tog; rep from *, ending k1 if 1 st rem after k2tog of last rep.

Row 16: K1, purl to last st, k1.

Rows 17–24: Rep Rows 13–16 two times—1 st inc'd each in Rows 17 and 21.

Rep the last 24 rows 9 more times—75 sts.

Center Section

Row 1: (RS) K1, k1f&b, knit to end—76 sts.

Rows 2–12: Work 11 rows in garter st, beg and ending with a WS row.

Decrease Section

Work garter and eyelet patt while dec at beg of RS rows as foll:

Row 1: K1, k2tog, knit to end—1 st dec'd.

Row 2: K1, purl to last st, k1.

Row 3: K2, *yo, k2tog; rep from *, ending k1 if 1 st rem after k2tog of last rep.

Row 4: K1, purl to last st, k1.

Rows 5–12: Rep Rows 1–4 two times—1 st dec'd in each of Rows 5 and 9.

Row 13: (RS) K1, k2tog, knit to end—1 st dec'd.

Rows 14–16: Knit.

Rows 17–24: Rep Rows 13–16 two times—1 st dec'd each in Rows 17 and 21.

Rep the last 24 rows 11 more times—4 sts rem.

BO all sts knitwise.

Finishing

Weave in loose ends.

Fill a sink with water and a small amount of detergent. Submerge the scarf, letting the water soak into the fibers evenly. Rinse, being careful not to agitate the fibers. Gently squeeze out as much water as you can. Lay the scarf out on several towels or a blocking mat. Using blocking wires, block so center section measures 13" (33 cm) wide, piece measures 6" (15 cm) long from CO to end of double-layer channel, 32" (81.5 cm) long in increase section, 1½" (3.8 cm) long in center section, and 38½" (98 cm) long in decrease section—78" (198 cm) total from CO to BO. Let air-dry thoroughly before removing blocking wires.

Two-Tone Brioche

DESIGNED BY ANN BUDD

Beginning with a provisional cast-on, **Ann Budd** combined rust and burgundy laceweight yarn in a two-color brioche pattern to create a rectangle. She then twisted one of the needles and used a three-needle bind-off to join the two ends together. The resulting mobius strip has neither a "right" nor "wrong" side, though one face is predominantly rust and the other is predominantly burgundy. A row of single crochet finishes the twisted edge while hiding any misshaped stitches. Knitted with larger-than-normal needles, this lofty cowl is featherlight.

FINISHED SIZE

About 9" (23 cm) wide and 26" (66 cm) long, before joining ends.

YARN

Laceweight (#0 Lace).

Shown here: The Verdant Gryphon Mithril (100% merino; 750 yd [685 m]/4 oz): Cadmus teeth (rust; LC) and moët & chandon-white star (burgundy; DC), 1 skein each.

Note: This is enough yarn to make two cowls.

NEEDLES

Size U.S. 4 (3.5 mm): set of 2 double-pointed (dpn) 7" (18 cm) or longer.

Adjust needle size if necessary to obtain the correct gauge.

NOTIONS

Size E/4 (3.5 mm) crochet hook; waste yarn for provisional cast-on; spare needle same size or smaller than main needles for three-needle bind-off; tapestry needle.

GAUGE

26 sts and 60 rows (counted as 30 rows in a light-side knit column) = 4" (10 cm) in two-color brioche patt.

design techniques

Two-color brioche stitch, pages 48 and 52.

Worked flat and joined into a twisted tube, page 146.

Provisional cast-on, page 164.

Three-needle bind-off, page 162.

Single crochet edging, page 166.

stitch guide

DS: Dark side of work; dark color forms the knit columns.

LS: Light side of work; light color forms the knit columns.

DC: Dark color; use dark-colored yarn.

LC: Light color; use light-colored yarn.

Sl1yo: Holding working yarn in front, sl 1 purlwise while bringing yarn to back to form a sl1/yo pair.

Brk1: K1 (the slipped st of the previous row) tog with its accompanying yo.

Brp1: P1 (the slipped st of the previous row) tog with its accompanying yo.

notes

○ A 16" (40 cm) circular needle can be substituted for double-pointed needles, but it is easier to slide the stitches to the other end of a double-pointed needle.

○ See About Brioche Knitting on page 52 for an explanation on working two-color brioche.

○ Every row of the pattern either begins or ends with "sl1yo"; be careful that the yarnover does not fall off the needle and be sure to work the yo with its companion stitch as part of the brk1 or brp1 on the following row.

○ You can make a longer, looser cowl by working more rows before joining the ends; doing so will require more yarn.

Cowl

With LC and waste yarn, use the crochet-chain method (see Glossary) to provisionally CO 60 sts.

Set-up row: With same side still facing, slide sts to opposite needle tip and join DC. With DC, *Sl1yo, (see Stitch Guide) p1; rep from *. Turn work.

Row 1: (DS LC; forms LC purl columns) With LC, *sl1yo, brp1 (see Stitch Guide); rep from *. Do not turn work.

Row 2: (DS DC; forms DC knit columns) Slide sts to opposite end of needle and pick up DC. With DC, *brk1 (see Stitch Guide), sl1yo; rep from *. Taking care to maintain last yo on needle, turn work.

Row 3: (LS LC; forms LC knit columns) With LC, *brk1, sl1yo; rep from *. Do not turn work.

Row 4: (LS DC; forms DC purl columns) Slide sts to opposite end of needle and pick up DC. With DC, *sl1yo, brp1; rep from *, taking care to maintain the LC yo of the last st for a proper brp1. Turn work.

Rep Rows 1–4 (do not rep set-up row) until piece measures about 26" (66 cm), ending with Row 1 (DS LC).

Finishing

Carefully remove waste yarn from provisional CO and place the 60 exposed sts onto the spare needle. Flip one needle to put a half-twist in the fabric, then hold the needles together and parallel with the needle holding the CO sts in the back and the needle holding the live sts of the last row in front—LC will be at right tip of front needle.

With LC, main needle, and working each sl1yo as a single st (as for brpl), use the three-needle method (see Glossary) to BO all sts knitwise, using Jeny's surprisingly stretchy method (see Glossary) to add a yo before every k2tog stitch.

With LC and crochet hook, join yarn at three-needle BO "seam." Working 1 single crochet (sc; see Glossary) in each brk1 edge st (that is, every other row), work 1 rnd of sc all the way around the cowl. Join with a slipstitch to beg of edging, and fasten off last st.

Weave in loose ends as invisibly as possible. Blocking is not necessary.

Design Notebook

Because they're worn draped around the neck and shoulders rather than fitting the arms and torso, scarves are an ideal place to set out on your own as a designer. Unlike garments in which a particular gauge has to be matched for the piece to fit, there's a lot of flexibility when it comes to scarves—or shawls, cowls, stoles, and wraps for that matter. You're free to focus on just the combination of yarn, needle size, shape, and stitch pattern. Although the possibilities are seemingly endless, there are some general guidelines that will help ensure success. Whether it's designed for warmth or decoration (or both, of course!), any neckwear should have sufficient fluidity to drape around the neck in gentle waves or folds, and the fabric should be comfortable against sensitive skin. But beyond these loose constraints, there are few elements that constitute a good design.

Getting Started

Just like any other garment, every scarf (or shawl, cowl, stole, or wrap) begins with yarn and needles. Thoughtful choices at the beginning will make the knitting as pleasurable as the wearing.

Yarn

Yarn choice is paramount to the outcome of any scarf and plays a large role in how much pleasure you'll take in knitting it. Almost any yarn can be used for a scarf, but the softer, the better. All other things being equal, soft yarns tend to drape better than coarse ones and they're much more likely to feel sumptuous against bare skin. With so many exquisitely soft yarns available today—including merino, alpaca, silk, and cashmere—it's hard not to fall in love. And because scarves tend to be relatively small, they are ideal candidates for those single skeins of luxury yarn purchased in moments of fiber passion.

Needle Size

The size of needle you pair with any chosen yarn will determine the ultimate density of the fabric. Use larger needles (a loose gauge) for a light, airy openwork fabric; use smaller needles (a tight gauge) for a thick, windproof one. It's not unusual for scarves, et cetera, to be knitted with needles that don't match the size (or the gauge) recommended on the yarn ball band. Play around with needle sizes to find the fabric that you like best. But as you do, be aware that the needle size will affect the finished dimensions as well as the amount of yarn you'll need.

Choosing a Shape

You can get the same shape a number of ways.

Most commonly, scarves are knitted as long, flat rectangles, beginning with the cast-on at one short edge and ending with the bind-off at the other. This most basic shape was chosen for Jared Flood's Cottage Scarf (page 27), Nancy Marchant's Brioche Branches (page 46), Véronik Avery's Pleated Chevrons (page 58), and JoLene Treace's Deep Shade Scarf (page 86).

Keep in mind that you can achieve the same basic shape a variety of ways. For Winter Garden Wrap (page 90), Rosemary (Romi) Hill began with a center square, then worked outward for the two "tails." Melissa Wehrle combined two weights of yarn and worked tucks along the center panel to add an interesting third dimension to Shadow Play (page 100). Although the center section is rectangular in shape, Galina Khmeleva tapered the short ends to points in her Star Palatine (page 66). It just takes a little imagination to come up with interesting ways to vary a standard shape.

For extra warmth and ease of knitting, try working the scarf circularly as a long tube, such as Lucinda Guy's Queenie (page 10), Deborah Newton's Tubular Fair Isle (page 76), and Courtney Kelley's Sylvie Scarf (page 82).

Limited Yarn; Limited Time?

If you have only a single skein of yarn and are short on time, try one of the following one-skein projects:

○ Passing Through Shawl by Debbi Stone (page 32).

○ Cable-Edged Shawlette by Connie Chang Chinchio (page 104).

○ Duplex (in the small size) by Laura Nelkin (page 118).

○ Ring of Roses by Evelyn A. Clark (page 123).

○ Airy Lace Scarf by Angela Tong (page 132).

If you have one skein each of two colors or two skeins of the same color, try one of the following two-skein projects:

○ Checkered Cowl by Olga Buraya-Kefelian (page 38).

○ Sea Spray Shawl by Angela Tong (page 42).

○ Cross Timbers by Alexis Winslow (page 62).

○ Deep Shade Scarf by JoLene Treace (page 86).

○ Shadow Play by Melissa Wehrle (page 100).

○ Ilme's Autumn Triangle by Nancy Bush (page 110).

○ Duplex (in the large size) by Laura Nelkin (page 118).

○ Two-Tone Brioche by Ann Budd (page 136).

Because this type of construction allows the floats and yarn ends to be hidden in the center of the tube, it is particularly nice for colorwork patterns—and as you knit, you always face the "right" side of the fabric. While Lucinda and Deborah each worked a single design around the full circumferences of their tubes, Courtney placed a different pattern on each side to add visual impact and knitting variety. She also slipped a single stitch at each "edge" to encourage her tube to lay flat. Deborah modified the overall rectangular shape by adding a garter-stitch triangle of single thickness at each end of her tubular scarf. Kathryn Alexander produces a third dimension by working a series of connected entrelac rectangles to form peaks in her Three-D Entrelac Scarf (page 20).

Of course, there are a lot of other shapes that make good scarves. One of the most popular among the designers in this book is a short tube that encircles the neck and has no chance of falling off. The easiest way to knit a tube is to cast on stitches for the full circumference and work in rounds for the desired length, which is the method used for Mags Kandis's Nordic Cowl (page 16), Evelyn A. Clark's Ring of Roses (page 123), Katya Wilsher's Textured Cables (page 96), and Alexis Winslow's Cross Timbers (page 62) and Eufaula (page 128). Except for Evelyn's Ring of Roses, all of these are worked straight from the cast-on to the bind-off edges. But Evelyn added a bit of shaping by increasing stitches in the allover lace pattern so that the bind-off edge has a larger circumference than the cast-on edge.

Another way to construct a tube is to work a flat rectangle, then join the cast-on and bind-off edges together. In this construction, the stitch pattern travels sideways across the circumference. Pam Allen used a three-needle bind-off to join the two edges in her Cable-y Cowl (page 54), while Olga Buraya-Kefelian used the Kitchener stitch for a more invisible join in her Checkered Cowl (page 38).

If a twist is added to the rectangle before the two short ends are joined, a mobius strip is formed that brings

another dimension to the tube. This type of construction is ideal for reversible fabrics because the "right" and "wrong" sides are on equal display, as in Laura Nelkin's Duplex (page 118) and Ann Budd's Two-Tone Brioche (page 136).

Another popular shape is the triangle, which, depending on the scale, runs the gamut between shawl and neckerchief. The generous proportions of Debbi Stone's triangular Passing Through Shawl (page 32) envelop the entire upper torso. A bit smaller in size, Angela Tong's Sea Spray Shawl (page 42) and Nancy Bush's Ilme's Autumn Triangle (page 110) hang about the shoulders. Despite its relatively oversized length, Angela Tong's Airy Lace Scarf (page 132) drapes around the neck more like a scarf than a shawl.

On the smaller end of the spectrum are Melissa Goodale's Green Cables (page 6) and Connie Chang Chinchio's Cable-Edged Shawlette (page 104), both of which form gentle arcs that encircle the tops of the shoulders.

Direction of Knitting

The direction of knitting will determine the orientation of the stitch pattern.

Whatever the shape of your scarf, you have choices in the direction in which to knit it—vertically (top to bottom or bottom to top), horizontally (side to side), or radially (outward from the center or inward from the edges). See pages 144–147 for general guidelines for different construction methods.

Most of the projects in this book were knitted vertically so that the rows (or rounds) of knitting progress from the bottom to the top, or vice versa. In **rectangular construction**—whether worked flat in rows or

Sea Spray Shawl, page 42.

cylindrically in rounds—this involves the simple approach of casting on at one short end, knitting for the desired length, then binding off at the other short end. If the stitch or color pattern is symmetrical along the vertical (row) direction, as Véronik Avery's Pleated Chevrons (page 58), Deborah Newton's Tubular Fair Isle (page 76), and JoLene Treace's Deep Shade Scarf (page 86), the top is not distinguishable from the bottom. If the stitch or color pattern is directional, however, it will appear "right side up" on one tail and "upside down" on the other.

To knit a short tube vertically, stitches are cast on for the full circumference, knitted for the desired length, then bound off all at once. If the pattern is symmetrical, as in Katya Wilsher's Textured Cables (page 96) and Alexis Winslow's Cross Timbers (page 62), it makes no difference if the cast-on edge is at the top or bottom as the piece is worn. Evelyn A. Clark added "invisible" shaping to Ring of Roses (page 123) so that the circumference expands from a narrow cast-on edge to a wider bind-off edge.

A triangle can be worked vertically from the point at the base to the wide side at the top or from the top to the base. There are a number of ways to work this shape. For her Sea Spray Shawl (page 42), Angela Tong chose the simple method of casting on a few stitches for the lower point, increasing systematically to the desired width of the long edge at the top, then binding off. Another option is to cast on stitches for the entire long edge at the top, then decrease systematically to the point at the base. Nancy Bush took a slightly different approach for Ilme's Autumn Triangle (page 110) and cast on stitches for the two short sides, then worked decreases in such a way to fill in the center of the shawl and end with just a few stitches at the neck. While progress is slow for the first few inches, it increases exponentially as decreases are worked and rows get shorter. For her Passing Through Shawl (page 32), Debbi Stone worked in the opposite direction—she cast on relatively few stitches at the neck edge, then increased to the combined width of the two short sides at the base before binding off.

In **horizontal construction,** the stitch columns are aligned perpendicular to the length of the scarf. For a rectangle, stitches are cast on for one long edge, worked the length of a short edge, then bound off along the other long edge. To work a triangle horizontally, as for Angela Tong's Airy Lace Scarf (page 132), stitches are cast on at the tip of one long edge (tail), increased to the apex, then decreased to the tip of the other tail.

In **radial construction,** stitches can be worked inward from the edges or outward from the center. To shape a rectangle this way, you can cast on stitches for each tail and work the tails for the desired length, then join the two pieces together at the center with the Kitchener stitch or a three-needle bind-off, which is the approach Kathryn Alexander took for her Three-D Entrelac Scarf (page 20). Alternatively, you can begin with a provisional cast-on at the center, then work each side outward. Rosemary (Romi) Hill modified this approach for her Winter Garden Wrap (page 90), which she began by knitting a square motif in the round for the center of the rectangle, then worked stitches outward from the square to form the two tails.

Construction at a Glance

Neckwear comes in a variety of shapes, and, depending on the direction of knitting, there are a number of ways to achieve each one. Consider the orientation of the stitches—and therefore the pattern—as well as the location of the cast-on and bind-off edges when choosing a knitting direction. The cast-on edges are denoted with heavy lines and arrows indicate the direction of knitting in the following illustrations.

FLAT RECTANGLE

Worked from Tail to Tail: Cast on for one short end, work for the desired length, then bind off for the other short end. The stitch or color pattern will flow continuously from the cast-on to the bind-off edge. This option is ideal for stitch patterns that look the same when viewed from top to bottom as when viewed from bottom to top.

See Cottage Scarf (page 27), Brioche Branches (page 46), Pleated Chevrons (page 58), Star Palatine (page 66), Deep Shade Scarf (page 86), and Shadow Play (page 100).

Worked from Side to Side: Cast on for the entire length, work for the desired width, then bind off. In this construction, the selvedges form the short ends and the stitch or color pattern will be arranged horizontally from one long edge to the other. Because the cast-on and bind-off edges are long, this option is a good choice for stitch patterns that create decorative scallops or points along both the cast-on and bind-off edges.

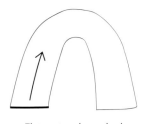

Flat rectangle worked from tail to tail.

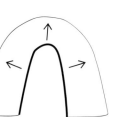

Flat rectangle worked from side to side.

Worked Upward from Each Tail: Cast on and work each tail separately, then join the two sets of live stitches with the three-needle bind-off or Kitchener stitch in the center. Use this option when you want the stitch or color pattern to appear right side up on both tails—it's especially good for patterns that create decorative scallops or points along the cast-on edge.

Worked Downward from Center: Use a provisional method to cast on for the desired width, work one tail to the bind-off edge, then rejoin the yarn at the provisional cast-on and work the other tail to its bind-off edge. Use this option when you want the stitch or color pattern to appear upside down on both tails—it's especially good for patterns that create decorative scallops or points along the bind-off edge.

See Winter Garden Wrap (page 90).

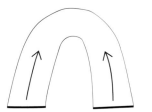 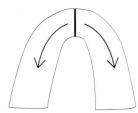

Flat rectangle worked upward from each tail.

Flat rectangle worked downward from center.

LONG TUBE

Worked from Tail to Tail: Cast on for the desired tube circumference (that is, twice the desired width), join for working in rounds, work for the desired length, then bind off. Use this option when you want only the right (public) side of the stitch or color pattern to be visible around the entire circumference and to flow continuously from the cast-on to the bind-off edge. It is best for patterns that look the same when viewed from top to bottom as when viewed from bottom to top.

See Queenie (page 10), Tubular Fair Isle (page 76), and Sylvie Scarf (page 82).

Worked Upward from Each Tail: Cast on for the desired tube circumference, join for working rounds, work to half the desired length, work a second piece to match, then join the live stitches of the two pieces with the three-needle bind-off or Kitchener stitch. Use this option when you want only the right (public) side of the stitch or color pattern to be visible around the entire circumference and you want the pattern to be oriented right side up along each tail. As for flat rectangles worked in this orientation, this is a good option for patterns that create decorative scallops or points along the cast-on edge.

See Three-D Entrelac Scarf (page 20).

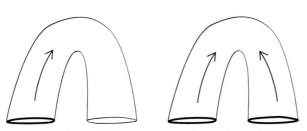

Long tube worked   Long tube worked
from tail to tail.   upward from each tail.

Worked Downward from the Center: Use a provisional method to cast on for the desired tube circumference, join for working in rounds, work one tail to the bind-off edge, then rejoin the yarn at the provisional cast-on and work the other tail to the bind-off edge. Use this option when you want only the right (public) side of the stitch or color pattern to be visible around the entire circumference and you want the pattern to be oriented upside down along each tail. As for flat rectangles

worked in this orientation, this is a good option for patterns that create decorative scallops or points along the bind-off edge.

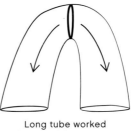

Long tube worked
downward from center.

SHORT TUBE

Worked from the Top Down (or from the Bottom Up): Cast on for the desired neck circumference, join for working in rounds, work for the desired length, then bind off. Use this option when you want the stitch or color pattern to be oriented right side up (or upside down). This method is particularly nice if the stitch pattern forms decorative scallops or points along both the cast-on and bind-off edges.

See Nordic Cowl (page 16), Cable-y Cowl (page 54), Cross Timbers (page 62), Textured Cables (page 96), Ring of Roses (page 123), and Eufaula (page 128).

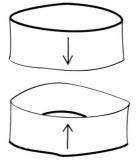

Short tube worked from the top
down (or from the bottom up).

Worked Flat and Joined into a Tube: Use a provisional method to cast on for the desired width, work for the desired length, then join the two short ends with the three-needle bind-off or Kitchener stitch. Use this option when you want a pattern to be oriented in the horizontal direction—it's particularly good for making horizontal bands appear as vertical stripes.

See Checkered Cowl (page 38).

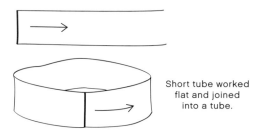

Short tube worked flat and joined into a tube.

Worked Flat and Joined into a Twisted Tube (Mobius Strip): Use a provisional method to cast on for the desired width, work for the desired length, twist the strip 180 degrees, then join the two short ends with the three-needle bind-off or Kitchener stitch. Use this option when you want the stitch or color pattern to be oriented sideways and so that both faces of the knitting will be visible—it's ideal for reversible patterns.

See Duplex (page 118) and Two-Tone Brioche (page 136).

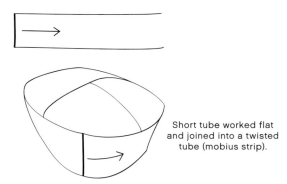

Short tube worked flat and joined into a twisted tube (mobius strip).

TRIANGLE

Worked from Bottom to Top and Shaped with Increases: Cast on a few stitches for the bottom point, then increase to the long edge at the top. Use this option when you want the stitch or color pattern to be oriented right side up. The advantage to this construction is that you can stop whenever you run out of yarn.

See Sea Spray Shawl (page 42).

Worked from Bottom to Top and Shaped with Decreases: Cast on for the desired combined length of the two short sides, then decrease to the long upper edge. Use this option when you want the stitch or color pattern to be oriented right side up and so that the cast-on edge extends along both short sides of the triangle—it's particularly good for stitch patterns that form decorative scallops or points along the cast-on edge.

See Ilme's Autumn Triangle (page 110).

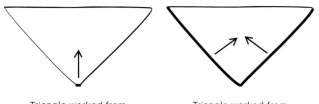

Triangle worked from bottom to top and shaped with increases.

Triangle worked from bottom to top and shaped with decreases.

Worked from Top to Bottom and Shaped with Decreases: Cast on for the desired length of the long edge at the top, then decrease to the point at the bottom. Use this option when you want the stitch or color pattern to be oriented upside down and so that the cast-on edge extends across the long side of the triangle. It's also good for stitch patterns that form decorative scallops or points along the cast-on edge, but, in this case, the scallops will be along the neck edge. The number of stitches cast on will determine the overall length of the triangle.

Worked from Top to Bottom and Shaped with Increases: Cast on a few stitches at the top, then increase to form the triangular shape, and end by binding off along the two short sides. Use this option when you want the stitch or color pattern to be oriented upside down and so that the bind-off edge extends across both short sides of the triangle—it's particularly good for stitch patterns that form decorative scallops or points along the bind-off edge.

See Passing Through Shawl (page 32) and Cable-Edged Shawlette (page 104).

Worked Side to Side: Cast on a few stitches for the tip of one "tail," increase along one side to the maximum width, then decrease along the same side until a few stitches remain for the other "tail." Use this method when you want the stitch or color pattern to be oriented perpendicular to the long edge.

See Airy Lace Scarf (page 132).

Green Cables, page 86.

CRESCENT

Worked from Top to Bottom (or Bottom to Top): Cast on stitches for the desired width of the shorter long edge, work in pattern for the desired length, working evenly spaced increases across a few rows to the desired width of the long edge, then bind off. Use this method when you want the stitch or color pattern to be vertically oriented and you want to space the shaping between narrow stitch panels instead of along the edges (or center back). This shape can also be achieved by beginning with the desired width of the long edge and working decreases to the desired width of the short edge.

See Green Cables (page 6).

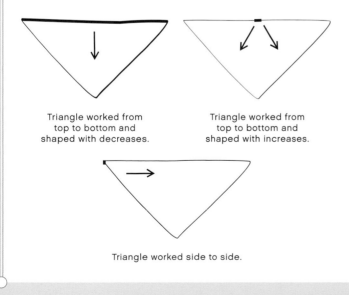

Triangle worked from top to bottom and shaped with decreases.

Triangle worked from top to bottom and shaped with increases.

Triangle worked side to side.

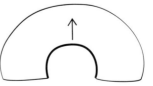

Crescent worked from top to bottom (or bottom to top).

Choosing Stitch and Color Patterns

Whatever the construction method, the real fun begins with choosing a stitch or color pattern. From subtle to bold and everything in between, the pattern(s) you choose will give your piece character and personality.

Cables

Work cables in reversible patterns
for the best on both sides!

Cottage Scarf, page 27.

Cables are worked by twisting two groups of stitches so that they exchange the order in which they are worked. In general, one set of stitches is placed on a cable needle, the next set of stitches is worked, then the stitches on the cable needle are worked. Depending on whether the first set of stitches is held in back or in front of the second set, the cable will lean to the right or left. Because cables involve overlapped stitches, they use up more yarn and draw in the knitting, which results in a narrower width than the same number of stitches worked in stockinette. However, the overlapped stitches trap more air and make for better insulation against cold and wind.

Cables are typically worked as knit stitches against a textured background, as in Jared Flood's Cottage Scarf on page 27 or the back panel of Debbi Stone's Passing Through Shawl on page 32, where stockinette cables are separated by narrow lace panels. An embossed texture is formed if the cables are worked against a plain stockinette background, as in the shadow plait cables in the tails of Lucinda Guy's Queenie scarf on page 10.

The stitches involved in cable crosses can also be worked in a combination of stockinette and reverse stockinette as in Katya Wilsher's Textured Cables (page 96), in a combination of slip-stitch rib and garter stitch as in Pam Allen's Cable-y Cowl (page 54), or in different rib patterns as for Melissa J. Goodale's Green Cables (page 6) and Connie Chang Chinchio's Cable-Edged Shawlette (page 104). While cables worked entirely in stockinette have a distinct right and wrong side, those worked in a combination of stitches can create a reversible fabric—a nice feature in a scarf or cowl that wraps and drapes so that both sides are visible.

When it comes to designing scarves, cable motifs can be repeated to form allover patterns (as in Green Cables, Cable-y Cowl, and Textured Cables), combined in panels (as in Cottage Scarf), or added as an accent or trim (as in Passing Through Shawl and Cable-Edged Shawlette). If the cable crosses occur near the cast-on or bind-off row or round, they will cause the edge to scallop attractively (as for Textured Cables).

Lace

For a light, airy fabric, work lace on needles larger than recommended for the yarn size.

Lace is produced by pairing yarnover increases with directional decreases to produce openwork holes, generally without changing the overall stitch count. To create an airy fabric, lace is often worked with fine yarn on needles larger than would be used to work the same yarn in stockinette stitch. After knitting, the fabric is stretched and blocked to reveal the beauty of the openwork design.

Lace stitches are a natural for scarves and shawls, whether they create open, delicate cobwebs or involve just a few scattered eyelets against a solid background. A simple strategy is to choose a single lace motif as an allover pattern, such as Angela Tong's Sea Spray Shawl (page 42) and Airy Lace Scarf (page 132) and the body of Connie Chang Chinchio's Cable-Edged Shawlette (page 104). When working with allover lace patterns, think about ways to incorporate the lace components into the structure and shape of the piece.

Don't be timid when it comes to combining lace patterns. If one pattern is nice, two, three, or more might just be divine. For her Ring of Roses cowl on page 123, Evelyn A. Clark stacked three similar lace patterns to create organic flare from the cast-on edge at the neck to the

Twisting Cables without a Cable Needle

Many cables, especially those involving four or fewer stitches, can be worked without a cable needle. This shortcut works best with "sticky" yarns that contain a significant percentage of wool; there is a greater chance of dropped stitches with slippery yarns such as alpaca or silk.

The illustrations here show a cable that involves just two stitches in which one stitch crosses the other. The same principles apply to cables worked over more stitches.

Step 1: Slip the first group of stitches (one stitch shown) off the left-hand needle and let it drop in the front of the work for a left-leaning cable or in the back of the work for a right-leaning cable.

Step 2: Slip the next group of stitches (one stitch shown) onto the right-hand needle to temporarily hold it, keeping the group of dropped stitches in front **(Figure 1)** or back, as desired.

Step 3: Return the group of dropped stitches onto the left-hand needle, then return the group of held stitches from the right-hand needle onto the left-hand needle **(Figure 2)**.

Step 4: Knit these two groups in their new order **(Figure 3)** to complete the cable.

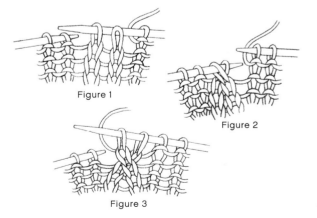

Figure 1

Figure 2

Figure 3

Star Palatine, page 66.

Other Texture Patterns

Stitch patterns that have about the same number of knit and purl stitches on the "right" and "wrong" side will lay flat and appear reversible.

bind-off edge at the shoulders. JoLene Treace aligned two lace patterns side by side in vertical panels separated by a bit of garter stitch for her Deep Shade Scarf (page 86). Galina Khmeleva repeated a small lace motif to make the assortment of larger diamonds and triangles that form the large center pattern in Star Palatine (page 66), and she edged the entire piece with a contrasting lace border. Rosemary (Romi) Hill chose to showcase a square motif in her Winter Garden Wrap (page 90), then she worked large leaf motifs along each tail. For Ilme's Autumn Triangle (page 110), Nancy Bush artfully stacked three distinct patterns to create an overall design that's arguably better than the sum of its parts.

In some cases, a little bit of lace goes a long way. Debbi Stone used narrow lace panels to set off the center back cable and add interest to the cable border in her Passing Through Shawl (page 32). Consider other ways that lace can augment or enhance another stitch pattern.

Don't overlook the way that most lace motifs result in beautiful undulations or points at the cast-on and bind-off edges, as well as along selvedges, all of which are on display in scarves and other neckwear. In most cases, these edges can be wet-blocked to hold their shapes.

In addition to cables and lace, there are many other ways to manipulate knit and purl stitches to create a variety of textural patterns that span the gap between bulky cables and airy lace.

Many texture patterns combine roughly equal numbers of knit and purl stitches on both right- and wrong-side rows to create fabrics that lay flat without curling, as well as fabrics that look nice on both faces. For examples, check out Olga Buraya-Kefelian's Checkered Cowl (page 38), Véronik Avery's Pleated Chevrons (page 58), and Laura Nelkin's Duplex (page 118).

Brioche stitch makes a unique type of reversible textured patterns. Worked by slipping alternate stitches at the same time as making a yarnover on one row, then working the slipped stitch together with its companion yarnover on the next row, brioche produces a lofty texture that resembles k1, p1 ribbing, but without the widthwise draw-in. This technique was used in Nancy Marchant's Brioche Branches (page 46) and Ann Budd's Two-Tone Brioche (page 136), both of which were worked in two colors so that the "right" and "wrong" sides have different, but equally pleasing, appearances.

Melissa Wehrle used tuck stitches to create a rippled effect along the center of Shadow Play (page 100) while the outer edges flair in gentle ruffles. She alternated two yarns of similar color but different weights and textures—a fingering weight silk/wool blend and a laceweight silk—to add to the visual appeal. Think of other ways to combine two (or more) yarns for textural effects.

Colorwork

Keep in mind that the more
colors there are, the more ends
there will be to weave in.

You can add exciting dimension to a design by including
a bit of color. Whether you choose to alternate stripes of
different colors or combine two or more colors in the same
row or round of knitting, you can get totally different
effects simply by changing the colors you use and their
juxtapositions. The biggest disadvantage to working with
multiple colors is that there will be more ends to weave
in. Because both sides of the fabric are usually visible in
scarves, this can be tricky. But the designers in this book
have come up with clever ways to minimize the problem.
Read on.

STRIPES

Carry the yarn along the selvedge
edge for two-color stripe patterns.

In general, stripes are the easiest way to add color.
Simply work the desired number of rows or rounds with
one color, drop that color, pick up a new color and work
the desired number of rows or rounds with that color.
Change colors as desired. Keep in mind that the more
colors you use, the more ends there will be to weave in.
But if just two colors are used, you might be able to carry
the unused yarn along the selvedge edge (if working in
rows) or along the "seam line" (if working in rounds), as
for Olga Buraya-Kefelian's Checkered Cowl (page 38) or
Melissa Wehrle's Shadow Play (page 100). Twist the yarns
around each other every couple of rows to keep the edges
tidy. This eliminates the need to repeatedly cut and join
new yarn, and the twisted yarns are only visible upon
very close inspection.

COLOR STRANDING AND FAIR ISLE

For the best results, be consistent in
how you hold the two yarns when
changing colors in Fair Isle patterns.

When two or more colors are used in the same row or
round of knitting, as for color stranded or Fair Isle patterns, the color that is not in use is carried or stranded
across the wrong side of the fabric. The strand adds a
second layer to the knitted stitches that makes the fabric
thick and insulating. To prevent puckers that can distort
the colorwork pattern, it's important to maintain even
tension between the various colors, both in the knitted
stitches and in the stranded lengths (also called floats).
For most people, this is easiest to do when working in
rounds because the right side of the work is always facing you and there are no purl rows.

For a simple tube, such as Mags Kandis's Nordic Cowl
(page 16) and Alexis Winslow's Cross Timbers (page 62),
a bit of the wrong side of the fabric is likely to be visible. For the best results, designate a "pattern" yarn and
a "background" yarn and be diligent in always picking
up the pattern yarn from under the background yarn and
always picking up the background yarn from over the
pattern yarn. Doing so will ensure that the floats form a
pleasing pattern of their own and the "wrong" side will
not distract from the "right" side as the cowl folds and
drapes around the neck.

When it comes to long scarves, these types of colorwork
patterns are most attractive when worked in narrow
tubes so that the floats are hidden in the center, as in
Deborah Newton's Tubular Fair Isle (page 76), Courtney
Kelley's Sylvie Scarf (page 82), and the colorwork sections
of Lucinda Guy's Queenie scarf (page 10). Keep in mind
that this type of construction will produce four layers of
fabric—two layers of knitted stitches and two layers of

stranded floats. The result is exceptionally warm and, in most cases, wind resistant. As with striped patterns, the more colors you use, the more ends there will be to weave in. It's a good idea to weave in the loose ends soon after each color change so they are within easy reach.

ENTRELAC

A class all its own, entrelac forms tiers of small triangles and left- and right-leaning squares or rectangles that build one upon another. By alternating tiers of left-leaning and right-leaning motifs, a flat fabric is formed. Kathryn Alexander took this concept a step further for her Three-D Entrelac Scarf (page 20), in which she worked two consecutive tiers of right-leaning rectangles followed by two consecutive tiers of left-leaning rectangles in a tubular arrangement to produce three-dimensional peaks. Although the faceted look would be striking in a single color, Kathryn used twenty-five for a riotous visual treat. Experiment with other shapes and sequences for your own modifications.

Three-D Entrelac Scarf, page 20.

Combined Techniques

Mix and match cable, lace, colorwork, and other patterns for inventive and interesting looks.

You can mix and match techniques for even more design possibilities, but be aware that different patterns may have different gauges that can cause ripples or puckers where you might not want them. For patterns worked in horizontal bands, you can prevent this by changing the needle size or stitch count between contiguous patterns. Gauge issues aside, there's no limit to the ways that stitch and color patterns can be combined in a unified design.

Pleated Chevrons, page 58.

For Queenie (page 10), Lucinda Guy alternated bands of Fair Isle with bands of cable patterns. Because both techniques tend to draw in the knitting somewhat equally, the width remains fairly constant from the cast-on to the bind-off edge. Both Debbi Stone (Passing Through Shawl; page 32) and Connie Chang Chinchio (Cable-Edged Shawlette; page 104) chose to juxtapose comparatively dense cables with openwork lace for an interesting play of texture. To showcase the lace panels in her Deep Shade Scarf (page 86), JoLene Treace positioned them between panels of relatively dense garter stitch.

Reversible Patterns

Make a pattern reversible by working it in a closed tube.

Because both sides of a scarf are usually visible when it is wrapped around a neck, reversible patterns are especially appropriate. In the simplest form, reversible patterns stem from designs that have roughly the same number of knit and purl stitches on each side of the fabric.

For her Checkered Cowl (page 38), Olga Buraya-Kefelian alternated rows of knits and purls in such a way that stockinette stitch alternates with reverse stockinette stitch. She added interest by alternating six-row stripes of two colors, then dropping every sixth stitch to superimpose a vertical element on the horizontal stripes. Véronik Avery also alternated knit and purl stitches in a chevron pattern punctuated by elongated slipped stitches to create a reversible hinged appearance in Pleated Chevrons (page 58). To make her Duplex (page 118) mobius cowl reversible, Laura Nelkin worked short-row "wedges" of garter and stockinette stitch. Similarly, Angela Tong paired garter stitch with eyelets to make both sides of her Airy Lace Scarf (page 132) attractive.

Although cables are typically thought of as twisted stockinette stitches against a reverse stockinette background, if those twisted stitches are worked in a combination of knit and purl stitches, the cables become reversible. Check out the way Melissa J. Goodale used k4, p4 ribs to make both sides of Green Cables (page 6) look the same. The cables in Pam Allen's Cable-y Cowl (page 54) are a mixture of slip-stitch rib and garter stitch separated by two-stitch columns of reverse stockinette stitch. The result is a heavily textured pattern that looks great no matter which side faces forward. Likewise, Katya Wilsher achieved reversible rustic texture by twisting columns of stockinette stitches with columns of reverse stockinette stitches in Textured Cables (page 96).

Brioche stitch patterns create raised ribs in a reversible pattern that resembles embossed k1, p1 ribs. For the Two-Tone Brioche cowl (page 136), Ann Budd worked the pattern in two colors to make one face predominantly rust and the other predominantly burgundy. Joined as a mobius strip, both faces are visible in an interesting contrast of light and dark. Nancy Marchant took a more artful approach and worked the raised stitches in striking patterns that resemble traveling stitches to produce different patterns on the two faces of her Brioche Branches scarf (page 46).

Another way to produce a reversible fabric is to knit a closed tube, as in Lucinda Guy's Queenie scarf (page 10), Kathryn Alexander's Three-D Entrelac Scarf (page 20), Deborah Newton's Tubular Fair Isle scarf (page 76), and Courtney Kelley's Sylvie Scarf (page 82). In all of these cases, the floats and woven-in ends are hidden in the inside of the tubes. An alternative method would be to knit double length or double width, then fold the piece and join the edges with seams or crochet.

Edgings

Edgings can add a lot to a scarf design, particularly
for flat pieces that are knitted back and forth in rows.
If the edging pattern resists curling, it can serve two
purposes—as a decorative border around the central
design and as a means to keep the edges flat. In most
cases, edgings can be worked simultaneously with the
body of the scarf, eliminating the need to pick up stitches
and work the edgings later.

Among the simplest edging patterns is **garter stitch**,
which creates non-curling and reversible horizontal
ridges. It works as well along selvedges as for cast-on
and bind-off edges. Garter stitch borders the bind-off
edges of Angela Tong's Sea Spray Shawl (page 42) and
Connie Chang Chinchio's Cable-Edged Shawlette (page
104). Because these shawls were worked in opposite
directions, the bind-off edge is at the top of Angela's
shawl and along the bottom of Connie's. Garter stitch is
also used to border both the cast-on and bind-off edges
of Alexis Winslow's Cross Timbers (page 62) and Eufaula
(page 128), and all four sides of JoLene Treace's Deep
Shade Scarf (page 86). Deborah Newton worked garter-
stitch triangles to finish each short end of her Tubular
Fair Isle (page 76).

Ribbing also produces a nice edging. Because it's so
variable in terms of the number and ratio of knit and purl
stitches in each repeat, it not only prevents the ends from
curling, but it can be set up to flow organically in and out
of other stitch patterns. Notice how the cables grow in
and out of the ribbed edges in Melissa J. Goodale's Green
Cables (page 6) and Jared Flood's Cottage Scarf (page 27).
For a colorful twist, Courtney Kelley worked corrugated
ribbing along the cast-on and bind-off edges of her Sylvie
Scarf (page 82).

Deep Shade Scarf, page 86.

If you want a **smooth finish** along the selvedge edges, try
slipping the first stitch of every row. Doing so will create
a decorative chained edge, as in Véronik Avery's Pleated
Chevrons (page 58) and JoLene Treace's Deep Shade Scarf
(page 86). If you want the look of stockinette, work a few
stitches in k1, p1 ribbing along each selvedge. For slightly
rounded edges, work the first few and last few stitches in
I-cord, as in Jared Flood's manly Cottage Scarf (page 27)
and Melissa Wehrle's feminine Shadow Play (page 100).

From intricate openwork patterns to just a few simple
eyelets, **lace** is always a good choice for edging scarves
and shawls. For the simplest application, cast on or
bind off with an openwork pattern that creates decorative scallops or points, as in the cast-on edge of Nancy
Bush's Ilme's Autumn Triangle (page 110). Another choice
is to work a lace pattern along the selvedges, such as
the six-stitch eyelet pattern along each edge in Angela
Tong's Sea Spray Shawl (page 42) or the more compli-
cated sawtooth pattern that Galina Khmeleva worked all

around (and mitered at the cast-on and bind-off edges) of her Star Palatine (page 66). Laura Nelkin simply picked up stitches around the mobius strip of her Duplex (page 118) and worked a narrow, yet reversible, eyelet lace pattern. Another option is to attach an edging by picking up stitches along the desired edge(s), then working a relatively narrow lace pattern, joining the two by working the last stitch of the edging together with one picked-up stitch every right-side row, much the same as attached I-cord (see Glossary), but working wrong-side as well as right-side rows.

Don't overlook **cables** as a nice way to trim an edge. Follow the same method used to attach a lace edging, only work the stitches in one of the many cable patterns. This is the method Debbi Stone used to attach a 10-stitch cable/lace motif along the long edge of her Passing Through Shawl (page 32). Connie Chang Chinchio used a reversible k1, p1 cable in her Cable-Edged Shawlette (page 104).

For a simple edging, consider **crochet**. Mags Kandis topped off her Nordic Cowl (page 16) with a contrasting crochet frill and Ann Budd worked single crochet around the edge of her Two-Tone Brioche mobius (page 136). Consult the many books of crochet patterns for other ideas.

Of course, you can forego the edging altogether if you chose to work the piece in a non-curling pattern, such as the bands of stockinette and reverse stockinette in Olga Buraya-Kefelian's Checkered Cowl (page 38), the brioche pattern in Nancy Marchant's Brioche Branches (page 46), the textural cables in Pam Allen's Cable-y Cowl (page 54) and Katya Wilsher's Textured Cables (page 96), and the bands of garter stitch and eyelets in Angela Tong's Airy Lace Scarf (page 132). There is also little chance of curling if the piece is worked as a long tube with the cast-on and bind-off ends finished off with seams, as in Kathryn Alexander's Three-D Entrelac Scarf (page 20).

The Importance of Details

Inasmuch as the right combination of yarn, needle, shape, and stitch pattern is necessary for a pleasing overall look, the details can elevate that look into a design that rivals the professionals.

Casting On and Binding Off

To prevent unwanted draw-in, choose cast-ons and bind-offs that can be blocked to the same width as the body.

Whether you cast on stitches for a short or long edge or work vertically, horizontally, or outward from the center, you'll want to be sure to use a technique that allows the cast-on edge to have the same lateral elasticity as the rest of the knitting. Otherwise, the edge will pull in and distort the stitches in the first few rows.

Good candidates for cast-ons are the long-tail, knitted, cable, tubular, and provisional, all of which are included in the Glossary that begins on page 160. To ensure sufficient elasticity in the cast-on edge, leave about ¼" (6 mm) of space between each stitch as you cast on using the long-tail, knitted, or cable methods.

The same is true of the bind-off edge—keep the stitches loose, but not sloppy. If you're concerned that the bind-off may be too tight, use a needle one or two sizes larger when working the standard method or use an elastic method such as the suspended, decrease, or Jeny's surprisingly stretchy bind-off, all of which are included in the Glossary.

Keep in mind that you can add a lot of pizzazz with decorative techniques, such as the picot method Lucinda Guy used to cast on the tails of Queenie (page 10) and the picot method Evelyn A. Clark used to bind off the wide edge of Ring of Roses (page 123). You can find a lot of other interesting cast-ons and bind-offs in knitting technique books and videos. Check out the Bibliography on page 174 for starters.

Shaping

INCREASES

Yarnover increases will create decorative holes; other types of increases will create more solid fabrics.

If you choose to shape your scarf or shawl with increases, keep in mind that you'll want to end up with full pattern repeats for pattern continuity. Because it can be tricky to increase stitches within a stitch pattern, you may find it helpful to chart the entire piece before you begin so you'll have a road map of how each increase will work into the next row of pattern.

There are a variety of increases to choose from. See the Glossary that begins on page 160 for the types that were used in this book.

For an open and lacy look, many designers chose to shape their pieces with yarnover increases. Galina Khmeleva placed yarnovers at each side of the center section in every right-side row to shape the point at the beginning of her Star Palatine (page 66). Angela Tong also worked yarnovers at each end of every other row to produce the triangle shape in her Sea Spray Shawl (page 42). For a faster rate of increases, Debbi Stone placed yarnovers at each selvedge as well as on each side of the central panel of her Passing Through Shawl (page 32).

Ring of Roses, page 123.

For Ring of Roses (page 123), Evelyn A. Clark camouflaged yarnover increases within the lace pattern for relatively invisible shaping from the narrower neck circumference to the wider shoulder circumference. Rosemary (Romi) Hill also used the yarnover increases inherent to the lace pattern to shape the center medallion of her Winter Garden Wrap (page 90).

For a more solid look, Connie Chang Chinchio used make-one (M1) increases at each side of each of the two lace panels in her Cable-Edged Shawlette (page 104). By working the increases at a faster rate (every row instead of every other row) at the outside edges, she created a gentle curve in each tail that helps the shawlette stay in place. Melissa J. Goodale opted for nearly invisible lifted increases to form the circular shape of her Green Cables (page 6). Neither completely invisible nor deliberately decorative, the bar increases in the first half of Angela Tong's Airy Lace Scarf (page 132) provide shape without distracting from the garter-stitch foundation.

Joining a New Ball of Yarn

When joining a new ball of yarn, use a method that is as invisible as possible.

Unless your scarf can be completed with a single ball of yarn, you'll eventually have to join a new ball of yarn to your knitting. With the exception of long tubes worked in rounds, both sides of a scarf are likely to be on display so you'll want to be careful to make the joins as invisibly as possible.

WET- (OR SPIT-) SPLICE

Untwist the plies for about 2" (5 cm) from the end of each ball **(Figure 1)**, break off about half of the fiber from each end, overlap the raveled ends **(Figure 2)**, and thoroughly moisten them with water (saliva works well and is readily available, if not always accepted in polite company). Place the overlapped loose fibers in one palm and use your other palm to vigorously rub them together **(Figure 3)**. The moisture and friction will cause the fibers to felt together and join the two balls together. Keep in mind that this method only works with yarns that are predominantly wool or other fibers that felt (superwash doesn't count).

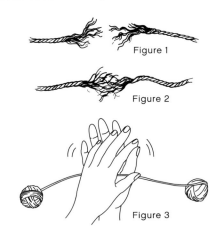

Figure 1

Figure 2

Figure 3

RUSSIAN JOIN

Thread the yarn from the old ball of yarn onto the smallest needle possible and pass the needle through the old yarn for an inch (2.5 cm) or so to anchor it **(Figure 1)**. Pull the tail through but leave an open loop to pass the new yarn through. Thread the new yarn on the needle, bring it through the loop in the old yarn, then pass the needle through the new yarn for an inch (2.5 cm) or so **(Figure 2)**. Pull both tails to tighten the join **(Figure 3)** until it is nearly invisible. Trim loose ends if necessary.

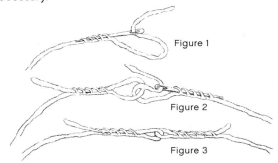

Figure 1

Figure 2

Figure 3

WORK THE TWO YARNS TOGETHER

A simpler, but less invisible, option is to leave a tail of the new yarn, work one stitch with the two yarns held together, then drop the old yarn and continue with the new yarn only. After several rows have been worked (or during the finishing process), thread the tails on a tapestry needle and work them into the wrong side of the piece, tracing the path of a row of stitches or skimming the stitches along a diagonal path.

DECREASES

Use directional decreases
for a symmetrical look.

It's generally easier to use decreases to shape pieces worked in stitch patterns because you don't have to extrapolate how new stitches will fit into the established pattern. To help maintain symmetry, especially in lace patterns, it's a good idea to use directional decreases for shaping—left-leaning (ssk) at the beginning of rows and right-leaning (k2tog) at the end of rows. Nancy Bush used this strategy to shape Ilme's Autumn Triangle (page 110). Because Angela Tong's Airy Lace Scarf (page 132) is only shaped on one side, she achieved the shaping with just right-leaning (k2tog) decreases.

Blocking

Blocking smooths out uneven and misshaped stitches and encourages the knitting to lay flat and maintain the desired shape and dimensions.

Most projects, and lace ones in particular, benefit from blocking. There are various ways to block a knitted scarf, shawl, cowl, or wrap—the method to choose depends on the yarn fiber, the stitch pattern, and the amount of time you have.

STEAM BLOCKING

Unless the yarn label tells you otherwise, most yarns can be quickly blocked by steam. Lay the scarf on top of towels placed on a blocking surface, then pin out the corners and straighten the edges as necessary. Hold an iron set on the steam setting about ½" (1.5 cm) above the knitted

Ilme's Autumn Triangle, page 110.

Airy Lace Scarf, page 132.

surface and direct the steam over the entire surface (except ribbing). Move the iron slowly above the scarf—never touching it—to let the steam penetrate the knitting. Allow the scarf to air-dry completely before moving it.

You can get similar results by placing wet cheesecloth on top of the knitted surface and touching it lightly with a dry iron. Lift and set down the iron gently; do not use pressure or a pushing motion.

WET BLOCKING

Fill a basin with lukewarm water. Submerge the scarf fully, then push down gently to saturate the fabric. Let it soak for at least 20 minutes so that the water penetrates the core of the fibers. Gently squeeze (do not twist or wring) out as much water as you can. Roll the scarf in a colorfast towel and press firmly to blot out more water until the piece is no longer dripping wet. Lay the damp scarf on a towel placed on top of a padded blocking surface and use rustproof pins or blocking wires to shape the scarf, stretching lace as necessary to reveal the openwork pattern and stretching out points on chevron or scalloped edges. Allow the scarf to air-dry thoroughly before removing the pins.

WET-TOWEL BLOCKING

Run a large bath or beach towel (or two towels for larger projects) through the rinse/spin cycle of a washing machine. Roll the scarf in the wet towel(s), place the roll in a plastic bag, and leave overnight so that the knitted pieces become uniformly damp. Pin the damp pieces to a blocking surface and let air-dry thoroughly before removing the pins.

Add a Bit of Fun

Add tassels, pom-poms, fringe, embroidery, or crochet for a finishing touch.

Don't overlook the chance to add a bit of whimsy to whatever type of neckwear you design. For a retro look, try tassels or fringe. Deborah Newton finished the pointed ends of her Tubular Fair Isle scarf (page 76) with chunky mismatched tassels. Kathryn Alexander took poetic license with the fringe on her Three-D Entrelac Scarf (page 20) and trimmed the scarf with lengths of striped three-stitch I-cord. Consider multicolored tassels, pom-poms, and regular fringe for completely different looks.

Embroidery is a fast and fun way to add bits of color and texture after the knitting is complete. Mags Kandis enhanced the two-color Fair Isle pattern in her Nordic Cowl (page 16) with the strategic placement of contrasting French knots. Lucinda Guy played along and added French knots to the Fair Isle sections of her Queenie scarf (page 10). Don't overlook other ways to add an embroidered pop of color to your own design.

Nothing says "feminine" as well as a well-placed ruffle. To counter the rustic feel of her chunky Nordic Cowl (page 16), Mags Kandis worked a series of crochet chains into each stitch along the bind-off edge. Worked in a contrasting color, this dense frill adds color as well as a bit of girly-girl. Lucinda Guy added a similar look to the ends of Queenie (page 10) by beginning each tail with a decorative picot cast-on.

While attractive pins can solve the problem of scarves and shawls falling off the shoulders, sometimes it's nice to forego the need altogether. To keep her Airy Lace Scarf (page 132) in place, Angela Tong worked a clever slot at one end through which the other end can easily pass.

Glossary of Terms and Techniques

Abbreviations

beg(s)	begin(s); beginning
bet	between
BO	bind off
CC	contrast color
cir	circular
cm	centimeter(s)
cn	cable needle
CO	cast on
cont	continue(s); continuing
dec(s)('d)	decrease(s); decreasing; decreased
dpn	double-pointed needles
foll	follow(s); following
g	gram(s)
inc(s)('d)	increase(s); increasing; increase(d)
k	knit
k1f&b	knit into the front and back of same stitch
k2tog	knit 2 stitches together
kwise	knitwise, as if to knit

m	marker(s)
MC	main color
mm	millimeter(s)
M1	make one (increase)
oz	ounce
p	purl
p1f&b	purl into front and back of same stitch
p2tog	purl 2 stitches together
patt(s)	pattern(s)
pm	place marker
psso	pass slipped stitch over
pwise	purlwise, as if to purl
rem	remain(s); remaining
rep(s)	repeat(s); repeating
Rev St st	reverse stockinette stitch
rnd(s)	round(s)
RS	right side
sl	slip

sl st	slip stitch (slip 1 stitch purlwise unless otherwise indicated)
ssk	slip, slip, knit (decrease)
St st	stockinette stitch
st(s)	stitch(es)
tbl	through back loop
tog	together
WS	wrong side
wyb	with yarn in back
wyf	with yarn in front
yd	yard(s)
yo	yarnover
*	repeat starting point
* *	repeat all instructions between asterisks
( )	alternate measurements and/or instructions
[ ]	work instructions as a group a specified number of times

Bind-Offs

Decrease Bind-Off

Slip the first stitch, *knit the next stitch, then *knit these two stitches together by inserting the left-hand needle into the front of both from left to right and knitting them together through their back loops with the right needle (**Figure 1**), then return the resulting stitch to the left needle tip (**Figure 2**). Repeat from * for the desired number of stitches.

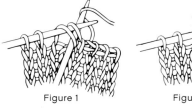

Figure 1   Figure 2

Jeny's Surprisingly Stretchy Bind-Off

To collar a knit stitch: Bring working yarn from back to front over needle in the opposite direction of a normal yarnover (**Figure 1**), knit the next stitch, then lift the yarnover over the top of the knitted stitch and off the needle (**Figure 2**).

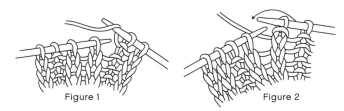

Figure 1   Figure 2

To collar a purl stitch: Bring working yarn from front to back over needle as for a normal yarnover (**Figure 3**), purl the next stitch, then lift the yarnover over the top of the purled stitch and off the needle (**Figure 4**).

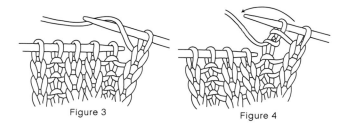

Figure 3   Figure 4

To begin, collar each of the first two stitches to match their knit or purl nature. Then pass the first collared stitch over the second and off the right needle—one stitch is bound off.

*Collar the next stitch according to its nature (**Figure 5**), then pass the previous stitch over the collared stitch and off the needle (**Figure 6**).

Repeat from * for the desired number of stitches.

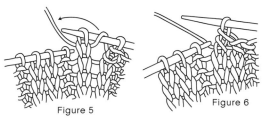

Figure 5   Figure 6

Sewn Bind-Off

Cut the yarn, leaving a tail about three times the width or circumference of the knitting to be bound off, and thread the tail onto a tapestry needle.

Working from right to left, *insert the tapestry needle purlwise (from right to left) through the first two stitches on the left needle tip (**Figure 1**) and pull the yarn through. Bring tapestry needle through the first stitch again, but this time knitwise (from left to right; **Figure 2**), pull the yarn through, then slip this stitch off the knitting needle. Repeat from * for the desired number of stitches.

Figure 1   Figure 2

Standard Bind-Off

Knit the first stitch, *knit the next stitch (two stitches on right needle), insert left needle tip into first stitch on right needle (**Figure 1**) and lift this stitch up and over the second stitch (**Figure 2**) and off the needle (**Figure 3**). Repeat from * for the desired number of stitches.

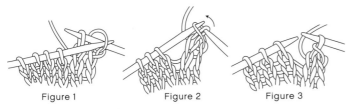

Figure 1   Figure 2   Figure 3

Suspended Bind-Off

Slip one stitch, knit one stitch, *insert left needle tip into the first stitch on the right needle and lift this stitch over the second, keeping the lifted stitch at the end of the left needle (**Figure 1**). Skipping the lifted stitch, knit the next stitch (**Figure 2**), then slip both stitches off the left needle—two stitches remain on right needle and one stitch has been bound off (**Figure 3**). Repeat from * for the desired number of stitches.

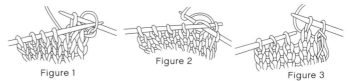

Figure 1   Figure 2   Figure 3

Three-Needle Bind-Off

Place the stitches to be joined onto two separate needles and hold the needles parallel so that the right sides of knitting face together. Insert a third needle into the first stitch on each of the two needles (**Figure 1**) and knit them together as one stitch (**Figure 2**), *knit the next stitch on each needle the same way, then use the left needle tip to lift the first stitch over the second and off the needle (**Figure 3**). Repeat from * until no stitches remain on first two needles. Cut yarn and pull tail through last stitch to secure.

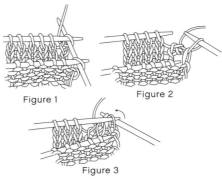

Figure 1   Figure 2

Figure 3

Tubular K1, P1 Rib Bind-Off

Cut the yarn, leaving a tail three times the circumference of the knitting to be bound off, and thread the tail onto a tapestry needle.

Step 1: Working from right to left, insert the tapestry needle purlwise (from right to left) through the first (knit) stitch (**Figure 1**) and pull the yarn through.

Step 2: Bring the tapestry needle behind the knit stitch, then insert it knitwise (from left to right) into the second stitch (this will be a purl stitch; **Figure 2**), and pull the yarn through.

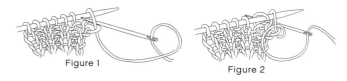

Figure 1   Figure 2

Step 3: Insert the tapestry needle into the first (knit) stitch knitwise and slip this stitch off the knitting needle (i.e., knit into the first st and slip it off the needle).

Step 4: Bring the tapestry needle in front of the first (purl) stitch, then insert it purlwise into the second stitch (this will be a knit stitch; **Figure 3**) and pull the yarn through (i.e., purl into the second st and leave it on the needle).

Step 5: Insert the tapestry needle into the first (purl) stitch purlwise and slip this stitch off the knitting needle (i.e., purl into the first st and slip it off the needle).

Step 6: Bring the tapestry needle behind the knit stitch, then insert it knitwise into the second stitch (this will be a purl stitch; **Figure 4**), and pull the yarn through (i.e., knit into the second st and leave it on the needle).

Repeat Steps 3–6 until all stitches have been worked.

Figure 3   Figure 4

TUBULAR K2, P2 RIB BIND-OFF

Set-up: After working k2, p2 rib for the desired length, work four additional rows by knitting the knit stitches and slipping the purl stitches while holding the yarn in front.

Cut the yarn, leaving about ½" (1.3 cm) of tail per stitch to be grafted. Place all of the knit stitches on one needle and all of the purl stitches on a second needle, being careful not to twist the stitches. Hold the needles parallel with the needle holding the knit stitches in front of the needle holding the purl stitches. Thread the tail on a tapestry needle and use the Kitchener stitch as described on page 169 to graft the two sets of stitches together.

Cast-Ons
Backward-Loop Cast-On

*Loop working yarn and place it on needle backward so that it doesn't unwind. Repeat from *.

Cable Cast-On

Make a slipknot of working yarn and place it on the left needle if there are no stitches already. Insert the right needle tip into the slipknot knitwise, wrap the yarn around the needle as if to knit, pull the loop through (**Figure 1**), and place it on the left needle in front of the slipknot (**Figure 2**). *Insert right needle between the first two stitches on the left needle (**Figure 3**), wrap yarn around needle as if to knit, draw yarn through (**Figure 4**), and place new loop on left needle (**Figure 5**) to form a new stitch. Repeat from * for the desired number of stitches, always working between the first two stitches on the left needle.

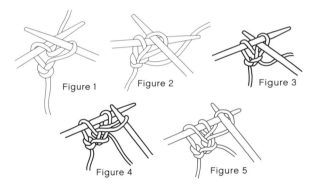

Figure 1   Figure 2   Figure 3

Figure 4   Figure 5

Crochet Provisional Cast-On

With waste yarn and crochet hook, make a loose crochet chain (see page 166) about four stitches more than you need to cast on. With knitting needle, working yarn, and beginning two stitches from end of chain, pick up and knit one stitch through the back loop of each crochet chain (**Figure 1**) for desired number of stitches. When you're ready to work in the opposite direction, pull out the crochet chain to expose live stitches (**Figure 2**).

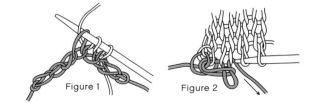

Figure 1   Figure 2

Emily Ocker's Circular Cast-On

Make a loose loop of working yarn. *Use a crochet hook to draw a loop of yarn through this loop, then draw another loop through the loop on the hook. Repeat from * for the desired number of stitches. Place the stitches on needles as specified. After a few inches have been knitted, pull the loose end to tighten the initial loop and close the hole.

Invisible Provisional Cast-On

Make a loose slipknot of working yarn and place it on the right needle. Hold a length of contrasting waste yarn next to the slipknot (or tie it together with the slipknot) and around your left thumb; hold working yarn over your left index finger. *Bring the right needle forward under waste yarn, over working yarn, grab a loop of working yarn (**Figure 1**), then bring the needle back behind the working yarn and grab a second loop (**Figure 2**). Repeat from * for the desired number of stitches. When you're ready to work in the opposite direction, place the exposed loops onto a knitting needle as you pull out the waste yarn.

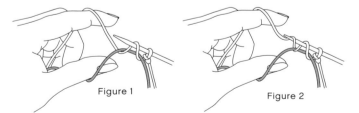

Figure 1   Figure 2

Tubular K1, P1 Cast-On

With contrasting waste yarn, use the backward-loop method (see page 163) to cast on half the desired number of stitches, rounding to the next odd number if necessary (the number can be adjusted after working the cast-on). Cut waste yarn. Continue with working yarn as follows:

Row 1: (RS) K1, *bring yarn to front to form a yarnover, k1 (**Figure 1**); repeat from * to end of row.

Rows 2 and 4: (WS) K1, *bring yarn to front, slip 1 purlwise, bring yarn to back, k1 (**Figure 2**); repeat from * to end of row.

Rows 3 and 5: Bring yarn to front, *slip 1 purlwise, bring yarn to back, k1, bring yarn to front; repeat from * to last stitch, slip last stitch.

Continue to work k1, p1 rib as established, removing waste yarn after a few rows.

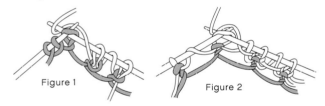

Figure 1   Figure 2

Tubular K2, P2 Cast-On

With contrasting waste yarn, use the backward-loop method (see page 163) to cast on half the desired number of stitches, rounding to the next odd number if necessary (the number can be adjusted after working the cast-on). Cut waste yarn. Continue with working yarn as follows:

Rows 1–5: Work as for k1, p1 tubular method at left.

Row 6: *K1, bring needle in front of first stitch, knit second stitch but leave this stitch on the left needle, p1 and drop both purl and knit stitches from left needle, p1; repeat from *.

Continue to work k2, p2 rib as established, removing waste yarn after a few rows.

Knitted Cast-On

If there are no stitches on the needles, make a slipknot of working yarn and place it on the left needle. When there is at least one stitch on the left needle, *use the right needle to knit the first stitch (or slipknot) on left needle (**Figure 1**) and place new loop onto left needle to form a new stitch (**Figure 2**). Repeat from * for the desired number of stitches, always working into the last stitch made.

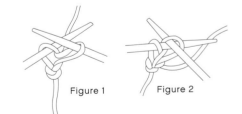

Figure 1   Figure 2

Long-Tail (Continental) Cast-On

Leaving a long tail (about ½" [1.3 cm] for each stitch to be cast on), make a slipknot and place on right needle. Place thumb and index finger of your left hand between the yarn ends so that working yarn is around your index finger and tail end is around your thumb and secure the yarn ends with your other fingers. Hold your palm upward, making a V of yarn (**Figure 1**). *Bring needle up through loop on thumb (**Figure 2**), catch first strand around index finger, and go back down through loop on thumb (**Figure 3**). Drop loop off thumb and, placing thumb back in V configuration, tighten resulting stitch on needle (**Figure 4**). Repeat from * for the desired number of stitches.

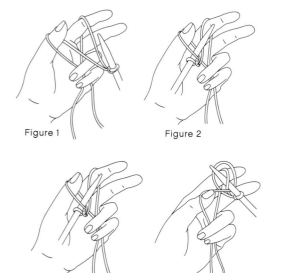

Figure 1   Figure 2

Figure 3   Figure 4

Crochet

Crochet Chain

Make a slipknot and place on crochet hook. *Yarn over hook and draw through a loop on the hook. Repeat from * for the desired number of stitches. To fasten off, cut yarn and draw end through last loop made.

Single Crochet (sc)

*Insert hook into the second chain from the hook (or the next stitch), yarn over hook and draw through a loop, yarn over hook (**Figure 1**), and draw it through both loops on the hook (**Figure 2**). Repeat from * for the desired number of stitches.

Figure 1   Figure 2

Slip Stitch Crochet (sl st)

*Insert hook into stitch, yarn over hook and draw a loop through both the stitch and loop already on the hook. Repeat from * for the desired number of stitches.

Decreases

Knit Two Together (k2tog)

This type of decrease slants to the right.

Knit two stitches together as if they were a single stitch.

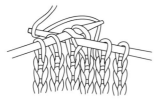

Slip, Slip, Knit (ssk)

This type of decrease slants to the left.

Slip two stitches individually knitwise (**Figure 1**), insert left needle tip into the front of these two slipped stitches, and use the right needle to knit them together through their back loops (**Figure 2**).

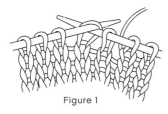

Figure 1   Figure 2

Embroidery

French Knot

Bring threaded needle out of knitted background from back to front, wrap yarn around needle three (or four) times, then use your thumb to hold the wraps in place while you insert needle into background a short distance from where it came out. Pull the needle through the wraps into the background.

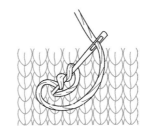

I-Cord

Standard I-Cord

This is worked with two double-pointed needles. Cast on the desired number of stitches (usually three to four). Knit across these stitches, then *without turning the needle, slide stitches to other end of needle, pull the yarn around the back, and knit the stitches as usual. Repeat from * for desired length.

Attached I-Cord

With the right side of the garment facing, use a separate ball of yarn and a circular needle to pick up stitches for the desired length along the garment edge. Cut the yarn, leaving a tail to weave in later. Slide these stitches down the needle so that the first picked-up stitch is near the opposite needle point. With a double-pointed needle, cast on the desired number of I-cord stitches. *Knit across the I-cord to the last stitch, then knit the last I-cord stitch and the first picked-up stitch together through their back loops. Pull the yarn behind the cord, then repeat from * until all of the picked-up stitches have been used.

Increases

Knit into the front and back (k1f&b)

Knit into a stitch but leave the stitch on the left needle (**Figure 1**), then knit through the back loop of the same stitch (**Figure 2**) and slip the original stitch off the needle (**Figure 3**).

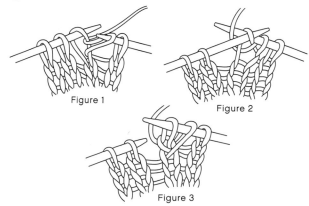

Figure 1

Figure 2

Figure 3

Raised Make-One (M1) Increase

With the left needle tip, lift the strand between the last knitted stitch and the first stitch on the left needle from front to back (**Figure 1**), then knit the lifted loop through the back (**Figure 2**).

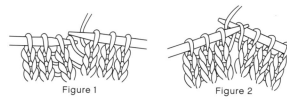

Figure 1

Figure 2

Yarnover

This type of increase is formed by wrapping the yarn around the right needle tip. The way that the yarn is wrapped depends on if it is preceded or followed by a knit or purl stitch.

BETWEEN TWO KNIT STITCHES

Wrap the yarn from front to back over the top of the right needle (**Figure 1**).

AFTER A KNIT STITCH AND BEFORE A PURL STITCH

Bring the yarn to the front under the right needle, around the top, then under the needle and to the front again (**Figure 2**).

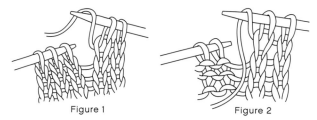

Figure 1

Figure 2

BETWEEN TWO PURL STITCHES

Bring the yarn from the front to the back over the top of the right needle, then around the bottom and to the front again (**Figure 3**).

AFTER A PURL STITCH AND BEFORE A KNIT STITCH

Bring the yarn from the front to the back over the top of the right needle (**Figure 4**).

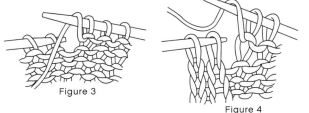

Figure 3

Figure 4

Kitchener Stitch

Arrange stitches on two needles so that there is the same number of stitches on each needle. Hold the needles parallel to each other with wrong sides of the knitting facing together. Allowing about ½" (1.3 cm) per stitch to be grafted, thread matching yarn on a tapestry needle. Work from right to left as follows:

Step 1: Bring tapestry needle through the first stitch on the front needle as if to purl and leave the stitch on the needle (**Figure 1**).

Step 2: Bring tapestry needle through the first stitch on the back needle as if to knit and leave that stitch on the needle (**Figure 2**).

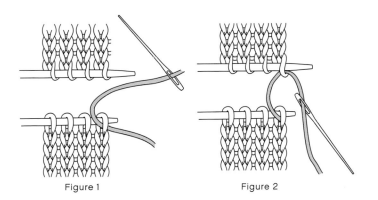

Figure 1

Figure 2

Step 3: Bring tapestry needle through the first front stitch as if to knit and slip this stitch off the needle, then bring the tapestry needle through the next front stitch as if to purl and leave this stitch on the needle (**Figure 3**).

Step 4: Bring tapestry needle through the first back stitch as if to purl and slip this stitch off the needle, then bring the tapestry needle through the next back stitch as if to knit and leave this stitch on the needle (**Figure 4**).

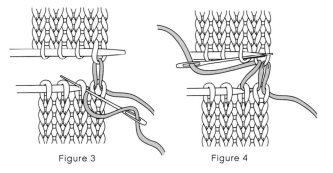

Figure 3

Figure 4

Repeat Steps 3 and 4 until one stitch remains on each needle, adjusting the tension to match the rest of the knitting as you go. To finish, bring the tapestry needle through the front stitch as if to knit and slip this stitch off the needle, then bring the tapestry needle through the back stitch as if to purl and slip this stitch off the needle.

Pick Up and Purl

With the wrong side of the work facing and working from right to left, *insert the needle tip under both legs of the selvedge stitch from the far side to the near side (**Figure 1**), wrap the yarn around needle, then pull a loop through (**Figure 2**). Repeat from * for the desired number of stitches.

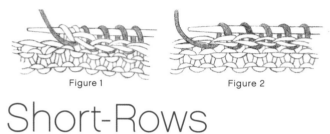

Figure 1   Figure 2

Short-Rows

Short-Rows Knit Side

Work to turning point, slip next stitch purlwise (**Figure 1**), bring the yarn to the front, then slip the same stitch back to the left needle (**Figure 2**), turn the work around and bring the yarn in position for the next stitch—one stitch has been wrapped and the yarn is correctly positioned to work the next stitch. To hide a wrapped stitch on a subsequent knit row, insert right needle tip under the wrap (from the front if wrapped stitch is a knit stitch; from the back if wrapped stitch is a purl stitch; **Figure 3**), then into the stitch on the needle, and work the stitch and its wrap together as a single stitch.

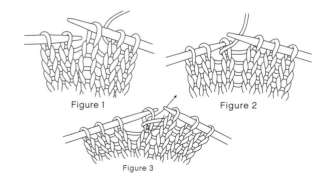

Figure 1   Figure 2

Figure 3

Short-Rows Purl Side

Work to the turning point, slip the next stitch purlwise to the right needle, bring the yarn to the back of the work (**Figure 1**), return the slipped stitch to the left needle, bring the yarn to the front between the needles (**Figure 2**), and turn the work so that the knit side is facing—one stitch has been wrapped and the yarn is correctly positioned to knit the next stitch. To hide the wrap on a subsequent purl row, use the tip of the right needle to pick up the wrap from the back, place it on the left needle (**Figure 3**), then purl it together with the wrapped stitch.

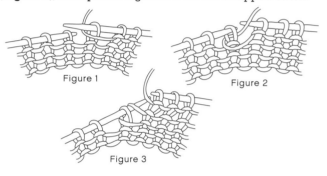

Figure 1   Figure 2

Figure 3

Tassel

Cut a piece of cardboard 4" (10 cm) wide by the desired length of the tassel plus 1" (2.5 cm). Wrap yarn to the desired thickness around the cardboard. Cut a short length of yarn and tie it tightly around one end of the wrapped yarn (**Figure 1**). Cut the yarn loops at the other end. Cut

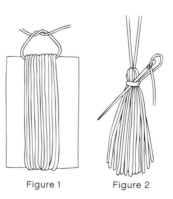

Figure 1   Figure 2

another piece of yarn and wrap it tightly around the loops a short distance below the upper knot to form the tassel neck. Knot securely, thread ends onto tapestry needle, and pull to center of tassel (**Figure 2**). Trim ends.

Contributing Designers

Kathryn Alexander (Three-D Entrelac Scarf, page 20) is a passionate spinner, dyer, and knitter who has brought three-dimensional entrelac knitting to the mainstream through her inventive patterns and kits. For a full selection of Kathryn's work, visit kathrynalexander.net.

Former editor in chief of *Interweave Knits* and creative director of Classic Elite Yarns, **Pam Allen** (Cable-y Cowl, page 54) is the founder of Quince & Company (quinceandco.com), which sources and manufactures yarns in the United States. Pam is author of *Knitting for Dummies* and the original *Scarf Style* and coauthor of *Wrap Style*, *Lace Style*, *Bag Style*, and *Color Style*.

Véronik Avery (Pleated Chevrons, page 58) is the author of *Knitting Classic Style* and *Knitting 24/7*, and the founder of St-Denis Yarns, which are sourced, manufactured, and distributed solely in North America. She lives in Montreal, Quebec. Learn more at veronikavery.com.

Olga Buraya-Kefelian (Checkered Cowl, page 38) learned to knit at her mother's knee at a very young age and now draws inspiration from industrial and architectural sources. Author of *Ori Ami Knits: Fiber Geometry* and *Shibui Silk*, Olga resides in Japan where she designs her own line of garments and accessories. Visit her at olgajazzy.blogspot.com.

Nancy Bush (Ilme's Autumn Triangle, page 110) is passionate about traditional knitting techniques, particularly those from Estonia. In addition to many books on sock knitting, Nancy is also author of *Folk Knitting in Estonia* and *Knitted Lace of Estonia*. Nancy teaches workshops in the United States and abroad and is owner of The Wooly West, a mail-order knitting shop (woolywest.com) in Salt Lake City.

Backed by a Ph.D. in physics, **Connie Chang Chinchio** (Cable-Edged Shawlette, page 104) is author of *Textured Stitches* and has contributed popular designs to numerous magazines and yarn companies. Connie lives in Jersey City, New Jersey.

A Pacific Northwest native, **Evelyn A. Clark** (Ring of Roses, page 123) is addicted to lace knitting. She is the author of *Knitting Lace Triangles*, and her designs have been published by numerous knitting magazines and yarn companies. You can find her work at evelynclarkdesigns.com.

Knitwear designer and photographer **Jared Flood** (Cottage Scarf, page 27) is the founder of Brooklyn Tweed (brooklyntweed.net), a small team of creative professionals committed to bringing handknitters high-quality knitwear designs and Brooklyn Tweed yarn.

Melissa J. Goodale (Green Cables, page 6) spends her days in Seattle dreaming up new designs and playing with yarn for her design company, Stick Chick Knits (scknits.com). Her projects expand to fill the space available, of which her loving husband and two sons are very tolerant.

Lucinda Guy (Queenie, page 10) is a knitwear designer-maker as well as the author of eight books, including *Northern Knits* and *Northern Knits Gifts*. She combines her love of folk art and traditional knitting techniques to create clothes, accessories, and toys for adults and children. Visit Lucinda at lucindaguy.com.

Rosemary (Romi) Hill (Winter Garden Wrap, page 90) is a knitwear and jewelry designer who gathers inspiration from her home in the high desert of northern Nevada. Lace is her passion and her work has appeared in numerous books and magazines. To learn more, visit designsbyromi.com.

Mags Kandis (Nordic Cowl, page 16) is a maker of stuff, designer of things, and author of *Gifted: Lovely Little Things to Knit and Crochet* and *Folk Style*, as well as numerous patterns for books and magazines. She lives in Consecon, Ontario. Visit magskandis.com.

Courtney Kelley (Sylvie Scarf, page 82) is co-owner of Kelbourne Woolens (kelbournewoolens.com), distributor of the Fibre Company's unique artisan yarns, and coauthor of *Vintage Modern Knits* and *November Knits*. Her designs have also appeared in *Knitscene, Interweave Knits, Interweave Crochet,* and *Vogue Knitting.* Courtney lives in Philadelphia.

Owner of Skaska Designs (skaska.com) in Fort Collins, Colorado, **Galina Khmeleva** (Star Palatine, page 66) has been teaching the art of Orenburg lacemaking across the United States since 1996. She is coauthor of *Gossamer Webs: The History and Techniques of Orenburg Lace Shawls* and author of *Gossamer Webs: The Design Collection.*

Born in Indiana, **Nancy Marchant** (Brioche Branches, page 46) now lives and works as a graphic designer in Amsterdam. She has written articles for *Vogue Knitting* and *Interweave Knits,* as well as a number of Dutch knitting magazines, and she is the author of *Knitting Brioche,* the first and only knitting book devoted exclusively to the brioche stitch. Learn more at briochestitch.com.

Although **Laura Nelkin** (Duplex, page 118) has a degree in apparel design, she took to knitting many years ago and hasn't looked back. When Laura is not designing or knitting, she is whipping up yummy feasts with her family, gardening, riding her bike, and taking time to play. Learn more about Laura at nelkindesigns.com.

Deborah Newton (Tubular Fair Isle, page 76) of Providence, Rhode Island, designs all kinds of knitwear for magazines and yarn companies, as well as fabrics for Seventh Avenue. She is the author of *Designing Knitwear* and *Finishing School: A Master Class for Knitters.*

Having learned to knit and crochet at an early age, fiber arts have always been an important part of **Debbi Stone's** (Passing Through Shawl, page 32) life. She lives in rural northwest Oregon where she chronicles her life, her family, and her designs at goddessknitters.blogspot.com.

Angela Tong (Sea Spray Shawl, page 42, and Airy Lace Scarf, page 132) lives in Brooklyn, New York, where she creates knitting and crochet designs. In her spare time, she likes to weave, spin yarn, sew, and bake. She is as passionate about crafting as she is about food. Follow her crafting and food adventures at oiyi.blogspot.com.

A professional member of the Association of Knitwear Designers, **JoLene Treace's** (Deep Shade Scarf, page 86) designs have appeared in a number of publications. She also self-publishes pattern leaflets through her business Kristmen's Design Studio.

Melissa Wehrle (Shadow Play, page 100) holds a degree in fashion design from the Fashion Institute of Technology and worked in the industry for ten years before deciding to dedicate her time to her own handknit design business. Her first book, *Metropolitan Knits,* is due to be published in 2013. You can see more of her work at neoknits.com.

Katya Wilsher (Textured Cables, page 96) lives in London, where she specializes in handknitted lace and textural garments and accessories. See more of Katya's designs at katyawilsher.com.

Alexis Winslow (Cross Timbers, page 62, and Eufaula, page 128) lives in Brooklyn, New York, and works as a printed textile designer. Between stitches, she keeps busy as art director and cofounder of the philanthropy organization CharitySub.org. Visit Alexis at knitdarling.com, where she shares her knitting adventures.

Sources for Yarns

Alpaca with a Twist
4950 S. White River Pkwy
W Dr.
Indianapolis, IN 46221
alpacawithatwist.com

Berroco Inc.
1 Tupperware Dr. Ste. 4
North Smithfield, RI 02896
berroco.com

Blue Moon Fiber Arts
56587 Mollenhour Rd.
Scappoose, OR 97056
bluemoonfiberarts.com

Blue Sky Alpacas
PO Box 88
Cedar, MN 55011
blueskyalpacas.com

Brooklyn Tweed
34 Danforth St., Ste. 110
Portland, ME 04101
brooklyntweed.net

Cascade Yarns
PO Box 58168
1224 Andover Park E.
Tukwila, WA 98188
cascadeyarns.com

Classic Elite Yarns
16 Esquire Rd., Unit 2
North Billerica, MA 01862
classiceliteyarns.com

Dream in Color
dreamincoloryarn.com

Elemental Affects
17555 Bubbling Wells Rd.
Desert Hot Springs, CA
92241
elementalaffects.com

Fleece Artist
fleeceartist.com

Hand Maiden
handmaiden.ca

Jojoland International
5615 Westwood Ln.
The Colony, TX 75056
jojoland.com

Kathryn Alexander Kits
PO Box 202
Johnsonville, NY 12094
kathrynalexander.net

**Kelbourne Woolens/
The Fibre Company**
2000 Manor Rd.
Conshohocken, PA 19428
thefibreco.com

**Knitting Fever, Inc./
Malabrigo**
PO Box 336
315 Bayview Ave.
Amityville, NY 11701
knittingfever.com

Misti Alpaca
PO Box 2532
Glen Ellyn, IL 60138
mistialpaca.com

Quince and Company
85 York St.
Portland, ME 04101
quinceandco.com

St-Denis
stdenisyarns.com

**Tahki Stacy Charles Inc./
Filatura di Crosa**
70–60 83rd St., Bldg. 12
Glendale, NY 11385
tahkistacycharles.com

**Universal Yarns/
Blossom St Cashmere**
5991 Caldwell Business Park
Dr.
Harrisburg, NC 28075
universalyarn.com

The Verdant Gryphon
verdantgryphon.com

Westminster Fibers/Rowan
165 Ledge St.
Nashua, NH 03060
westminsterfibers.com

Bibliography

From specific techniques to general stitch dictionaries, the following books will get you started on the right foot when it comes to designing your own scarf, shawl, cowl, or wrap.

Allen, Pam. *Scarf Style: Innovative to Traditional, 31 Inspirational Styles to Knit and Crochet*. Loveland, Colorado: Interweave, 2004.

Allen, Pam and Ann Budd. *Lace Style: Traditional to Innovative, 21 Inspired Designs to Knit*. Loveland, Colorado: Interweave, 2007.

Barr, Lynne. *Reversible Knitting: 50 Brand-New, Groundbreaking Stitch Patterns*. New York: STC Craft/A Melanie Falick Book, 2009.

Bestor, Leslie Ann. *Cast On, Bind Off: 54 Step-by-Step Methods; Find the Perfect Start and Finish for Every Knitting Project*. Storey, 2012.

Bush, Nancy. *Knitted Lace of Estonia: Techniques, Patterns, and Traditions*. Loveland, Colorado: Interweave, 2008.

Chin, Lily M. *Power Cables: The Ultimate Guide to Innovative Cables*. Loveland, Colorado: Interweave, 2010.

Clark, Evelyn A. *Knitting Lace Triangles*. East Wenatchee, Washington: Fiber Trends, 2007.

Dalvi, Anna. *Shaping Shawls*. Lakewood, Ohio: Cooperative Press, 2011.

Drysdale, Rosemary. *Entrelac: The Essential Guide to Interlace Knitting*. New York: Sixth & Spring, 2010.

Khmeleva, Galina. *Gossamer Webs: The History and Techniques of Orenburg Lace Shawls*. Loveland, Colorado: Interweave, 1998.

Knight, Erika, ed. *The Harmony Guides: Cables & Arans*. Loveland, Colorado: Interweave, 2007

———. *The Harmony Guides: Knit & Purl*. Loveland, Colorado: Interweave, 2007.

———. *The Harmony Guides: Lace & Eyelets*. Loveland, Colorado: Interweave, 2007.

Marchant, Nancy. *Knitting Brioche: The Essential Guide to the Brioche Stitch*. North Light Books, 2010.

Mucklestone, Mary Jane. *200 Fair Isle Motifs*. Loveland, Colorado: Interweave, 2011.

Walker, Barbara G. *A Treasury of Knitting Patterns*. Pittsville, Wisconsin: Schoolhouse Press, 1998.

———. *A Second Treasury of Knitting Patterns*. Pittsville, Wisconsin: Schoolhouse Press, 1998.

———. *Charted Knitting Designs: A Third Treasury of Knitting Patterns*. Pittsville, Wisconsin: Schoolhouse Press, 1998.

Index

Continue your knitting journey

WITH MORE INSPIRATIONAL STYLE SERIES RESOURCES FROM INTERWEAVE

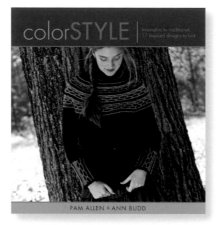

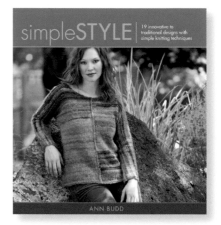

Scarf Style
Innovative to Traditional
31 Inspirational Styles
to Knit and Crochet
Pam Allen
ISBN 978-1-93149-954-5
$21.95

Color Style
Innovative to Traditional
17 Inspired Designs to Knit
Ann Budd, Pam Allen
ISBN 978-1-59668-062-3
$24.95

Simple Style
19 Innovative to Traditional
Designs with Simple
Knitting Techniques
Ann Budd
ISBN 978-1-59668-090-6
$24.95

Available at
your favorite retailer or

shop.knittingdaily.com

knitting daily

Join Knittingdaily.com, an online community that shares your passion for knitting. You'll get a free e-newsletter, free patterns, projects store, a daily blog, event updates, galleries, tips and techniques, and more. Sign up for *Knitting Daily* at **Knittingdaily.com.**

KNITS *INTERWEAVE*

From cover to cover, *Interweave Knits* magazine presents great projects for the beginner to the advanced knitter. Every issue is packed full of captivating smart designs, step-by-step instructions, easy-to-understand illustrations, plus well-written, lively articles sure to inspire. **Interweaveknits.com**